Creative Mathematics Teaching with Calculators

Also by David E. Williams

The MathMate Activity Books, Levels 1-3

Creative Mathematics Teaching with Calculators

Explorations and Investigations

David E. Williams, Ed. D.

STOKES PUBLISHING COMPANY
Mountain View, California

To Elaine, the giant in my life;

and to my giants in mathematics education:

Lola May, Evan Maletsky, Max Sobel and the late Julius Hlavaty,

all of whom unknowingly

pointed me in the right direction.

© 1992 by Stokes Publishing Company
2444 Old Middlefield Way, Suite M
Mountain View, California 94043

Printed in the United States of America

ISBN 0-914534-07-6

Contents

Preface   00

CHAPTER I **To the Teacher**   1

Introduction   1
Rationale for the Book   2
Overview of the Book   2
Recommendations of National Reports   3
    NCTM Standards   3
    Reshaping School Mathematics   4
Types of Calculators   5
    Basic or Four-Function   5
    Fraction   6
    Scientific   7
    Graphing   8
Summary   9

CHAPTER II **"Showstoppers"**   11

Introduction   11
Magic Addition and the Swami   12
7, 11, 13   16
1992 and Other Dates   18
What's the Pattern?   24
Problem Solving with "Little Numbers" or Exponents   26
Play It Again... and Again   31
    Hit the Target   35
A Percent Exploration   36
Summary   39

CHAPTER III **Mental Math**   40

Introduction   40
"Look Before You Leap"   41
Flash Cards   41
Quick Stuff   43
Warm-Ups   45
Competitions   46
One to Five   47
Summary   50

CHAPTER IV **Estimation**   51

Introduction   51
Estimation Derby   51
Be Reasonable   54
Order Please   55
Dot's Right   56
Summary   58

CHAPTER V **Number Crunching**   59

Introduction   59
Product Exploration   59
Ring Toss   62
Addition and Multiplication Trails   65
Million Madness   69
Summary   71

CHAPTER VI **Patterns**   72

Introduction   72
Two Digits from Three Digits   72
Nines and More Nines   77
Summary   80

CHAPTER VII **Recreations**   81

Introduction   81
The Division Game   81
Short Stuff   84

Missing Factor Game 86
Power Game 88
Summary 90

CHAPTER VIII **Word Fun** 91

Introduction 91
Words and Numbers 91
Problem Solving with Words 93
A Tall Tale 95
Crossword Power 97
Tongue Twisters 99
Summary 99

CHAPTER IX **Some Final Words** 101

A Look Ahead 101
Suggested Readings 102
Additional Sources 102

Preface

To borrow from a song from the popular musical, "The Sound of Music," this book is a "list of my favorite things." These "favorite things" relate to teaching mathematics using calculators. While this book is about the use of calculators, it could be about the use of the computer, exciting new laser-disk technology, interactive television, or perhaps, some years ago, about the introduction of the quill pen. Why? Because this book is more about affecting change in attitudes toward the use of calculators, and about the potential for teaching effective mathematics in the 1990's and beyond if these attitudes change.

In my travels doing calculator workshops for schools and districts throughout the United States, I see teachers using calculators and understanding the vision contained in The National Council of Teachers of Mathematics' Curriculum and Evaluation Standards for School Mathematics. Students in their classrooms are engaged in problem solving and pattern explorations using calculators. These classrooms are a joy to visit and are what the framers of the Standards envisioned in writing the Standards. But there is a significant number of teachers of mathematics at both the elementary and secondary levels who still are not using the calculator to assist them in the teaching of mathematics. Though this book has something for both of the above groups of teachers, it is my hope that it will have a positive affect on the attitudes of the latter group.

Creative Mathematics Teaching with Calculators focuses on teaching mathematics with calculators but also looks at the bigger picture of teaching mathematics. While showing teachers how to integrate calculator use in the classroom and actively involving students in the process of problem solving, it contains many suggestions for teaching mathematics in general.

This book will be labeled a methods book, but it is more than that.

It is meant to be read with enjoyment like a good novel. It is not a workbook. There are activities which you may want to use tomorrow morning but there are few, if any, pages that can be called worksheets for you to copy and distribute to your students. The book conveys an attitude about teaching mathematics and teaching with calculators; if you understand the message, you will become an even better teacher of mathematics.

David E. Williams

CHAPTER I

To the Teacher

INTRODUCTION

A combination of advanced technology and decreasing costs has made calculators more accessible to persons in all walks of life, including students in our classrooms. The use of calculators in classrooms and homes will give greater importance to the understanding of numbers and less importance to the learning of complex algorithmic processes. Calculators will not be a substitute for the learning of basic arithmetic skills but will create a necessity for greater emphasis on many arithmetic skills such as estimation and rounding numbers. Finally, the use of calculators has the potential to make applying mathematics to the solution of problems the major focus of our mathematics curricula.

I wrote the above paragraph in 1984 in the introduction to a book on how to use calculators, and the message contained in the above paragraph is as true today as it was then. I use it again here to provide a historical perspective on calculator use in classrooms. In the intervening years since the words were first written, there has been less resistance to using calculators to teach mathematics. Most teachers now see the obvious advantage of using calculators to teach mathematics. The major influence for the increased emphasis on the use of technology, including calculators, in classrooms is attributed to the recommendations contained in the landmark document, Curriculum and Evaluation Standards for School Mathematics published by the National Council of Teachers of Mathematics, and other national reports on mathematics education.

This is an exciting time to be involved in the teaching of mathematics. In light of increased support of mathematics education in the United States, there are many, many projects being developed to improve the teaching and learning of mathematics. These projects have the potential to positively change the curriculum, methods, and materials we use to teach students, and the procedures we use to assess student achievement. The operative word in the preceding sentence is "change." Change is difficult but necessary. This book is about change. It is more of a book on the teaching of mathematics in classrooms where calculators are available at all times rather than a calculator activity book. As you read through this book, you will understand the above statement and begin to use calculators on a daily basis to help your students learn mathematics.

RATIONALE FOR THE BOOK

This book was created with the concept of change in mind. This is not a comprehensive set of calculator activities, nor is it a book on how to use a specific calculator. It is limited to my favorite activities to use when teaching mathematics with calculators. Use of the activities and suggested extensions can help the reader develop an attitude toward calculator use, i.e., calculator use can be integrated into the teaching of mathematics to enhance those mathematics skills and concepts being taught.

The focus of the book is on rich explorations and discoveries in mathematics aided by the use of calculators. Over the years, I have led hundreds of workshops for thousands of teachers, supervisors, and parents and taught lessons using calculators for students at all levels of instruction. Repeatedly, I have been asked if the activities I used exist in any book. Each time I have been asked this question, I have pointed to my head and said, "It's up here." Now it is in this book.

OVERVIEW OF THE BOOK

This book is organized to help teachers develop a needed level of confidence to use calculators effectively. This first chapter contains information about the book and how to use it. The remaining chapters all follow the same format. Activities and investigations in these chapters are in three parts—prologue, procedure, and follow-up. The prologue part of each activity provides background information on the activity and suggested levels of use. Any prerequisite skills needed for successful use of the activity are also discussed. "Props" and other materials which may enhance delivery of the activity are also included. The procedure part of each activity suggests a script to follow in presenting the activity. Narrative in nature, it describes actual classroom experiences. The follow-up part includes extensions to try and anecdotes about use of the activity. In essence, the three parts of each activity constitute a "lesson plan."

With the exception of references to special features of specific calculators, all the activities in this book can be used with almost any calculator that is used in classrooms today-another example of the book's emphasis on teaching mathematics.

Chapter II contains a set of activities and investigations called "showstoppers"-seven motivational activities that deal with problem solving and pattern exploration. Mental-math activities are covered in Chapter III—students must be taught the appropriate use of calculators and that for many computations and situations, it is faster to use one's mind rather than a machine. Chapters IV deals with estimation activities. Students cannot use calculators effectively unless they can estimate. Chapter V covers activities involving large numbers and exhaustive searches and is entitled "Number Crunching." Chapter VI contains activities and explorations involving pattern searches. Recreations, the title of Chapter VII, contains several favorite games involving the use of calculators. Chapter VIII is a zany collection of "upside-down word" techniques. Chapter IX suggests a look ahead to how the technology may change and contains a list of references.

The "heart" of this book is problem solving and exploring patterns. Though specific chapters deal with both these subjects, various aspects of these topics are part of each and every activity.

The activities in this book are appropriate for teachers of students from elementary school to high school. While an activity on repeated addition may only be appropriate for primary students and for special populations, the message that is woven through all the activities is for all teachers of mathematics.

RECOMMENDATIONS OF NATIONAL REPORTS

NCTM Standards

The National Council of Mathematics' Curriculum and Evaluation Standards for School Mathematics offer a vision of what mathematics our students should be learning in a set of goals with a common philosophy and framework. The Standards specify five general goals for all students:

- Learn to value mathematics
- Become confident in their ability to do mathematics
- Become mathematical problem solvers
- Learn to communicate mathematically
- Learn to reason mathematically

The Curriculum Standards are articulated separately in sections for grades K-4, 5-8, and 9-12. At each of these three levels, underlying assumptions are described which helped in the shaping of the Standards. The use of technology, specifically the use of calculators, is an integral part of these assumptions. At the K-4 level, the curriculum "should make appropriate and ongoing use of calculators and computers." At the 5-8 level, "all students will have a calculator with functions consistent with the tasks envisioned in this curriculum." For grades 9-12, "scientific calculators with graphing capabilities will be available to all students at all times."

Furthermore, the overview to the Standards states a belief of the framers of the Standards that "appropriate calculators should be available to all students at all times."

Reshaping School Mathematics

The Mathematical Sciences Education Board and The National Research Council, who earlier published Everybody Counts: A Report to the Nation on the Future of Mathematics Education, have developed a common base for curriculum reform in Reshaping School Mathematics, A Philosophy and Framework for Curriculum. Citing the NCTM Standards and its earlier Everybody Counts as documents that have set the stage for curriculum reform in mathematics education, this exciting booklet "opens a door to a whole new vision of mathematics education."

The changing role of technology, specifically that of calculators and computers, is one of two important issues that form the base for the recommendations in Reshaping School Mathematics. In developing a rationale for change, the document states that "the changes brought about by computers and calculators are so profound as to require readjustment in the balance and approach to virtually every topic in school mathematics."

The document discusses the mathematical needs of citizens in an informational age and the lessening of the role of routine computation in school mathematics. With calculators and computers, teachers "can focus instead on the conceptual insights and analytic skills that have always been at the heart of mathematics."

In developing a practical philosophy for needed change in school mathematics, the document clarifies mathematics as the study of patterns as opposed to a "craft for calculation." In this light, an analogy is developed: "as microscopes are to biology and telescopes are to astronomy, calculators and computers have become essential tools for the study of patterns."

The vision inherent in the recommendations of the Standards and the framework for change contained in Reshaping School Mathematics recognize the potential of calculator use in our classrooms. It is in light of this vision that this book has been written. As we move toward "total access" to calculators at all times, the use of the material in this book will help you teach students to use calculators appropriately as they learn mathematics.

TYPES OF CALCULATORS

This book is about teaching mathematics with calculators. As such, the types of calculators mentioned in the text are limited to those that are used in classrooms. There are literally hundreds of calculators available to the consumer in electronic stores throughout the country, but those that are used in classrooms fall into only a few classifications.

Basic or Four-Function

This type of calculator is the one that is used in most elementary schools. It is referred to as a four-function calculator because it has the four basic operations (+, -, x, ÷) built into it. Most of these calculators also have memory and constant capabilities, as well as change sign, percent, square, and square root keys. These calculators have a logic system which processes operations from left to right regardless of the standard order of operations. The most widely used basic calculator in our schools today is the Texas Instruments TI-108. As with most calculators that are used in classrooms today, the TI-108 is solar powered.

A new basic calculator and the first that does adhere to the standard order of operations is the Texas Instruments MathMate. This calculator has AOS™ (Algebraic Operating System) which will perform multiplications and divisions before additions and subtractions. It also has

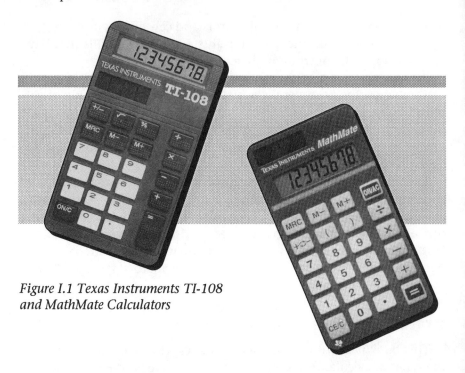

Figure I.1 Texas Instruments TI-108 and MathMate Calculators

parenthesis keys for overriding the standard order of operations. It does not have percent or square root keys and has been designed for use with young students.

Fraction

Touted by Texas Instruments as "the only calculator designed for teaching fractions," the TI-12 Math Explorer allows fractions to be entered, displayed, and manipulated. It has an algebraic hierarchy logic system and is solar powered. Fractions can be converted to decimals and vice versa. It performs integer division. It has a "fix" key that can be used to set the number of decimal places displayed. It has much more.

When teachers start playing with the Math Explorer, they quickly see the potential of this calculator to change the way mathematics is taught at the middle school level. Its many features eliminate the need to spend countless hours teaching computation with fractions and decimals and allow the teacher to concentrate on process and concepts. It is a powerful calculator for use with middle school students.

Scientific

All scientific calculators have an algebraic hierarchy logic system which adheres to the standard order of operations. In addition to the four basic operation keys of a basic calculator, all scientific calculators can perform trigonometric and logarithmic functions. Some scientifics also perform statistical functions. Other function keys may include the ability to compute reciprocals, and powers and roots. The solar powered TI-30 Challenger from Texas Instruments is a popular scientific calculator used in classrooms.

A calculator with full range of scientific functions and much more is the Texas Instruments TI-34. In addition to basic trigonometric and logarithmic functions, the TI-34 has one-variable statistical capability and a fraction feature that allows the input, display, and manipulation of fractions. In addition to calculating in the normal decimal notation, it can perform calculations in binary, hexadecimal, and octal number bases and perform logic operations in these bases.

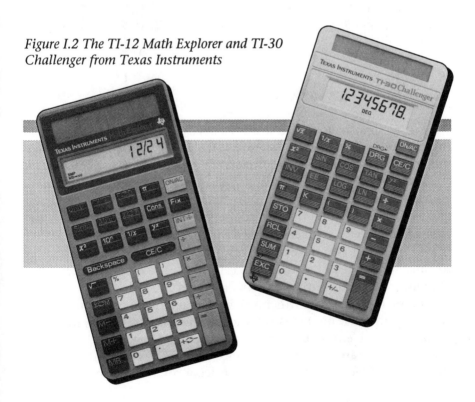

Figure I.2 The TI-12 Math Explorer and TI-30 Challenger from Texas Instruments

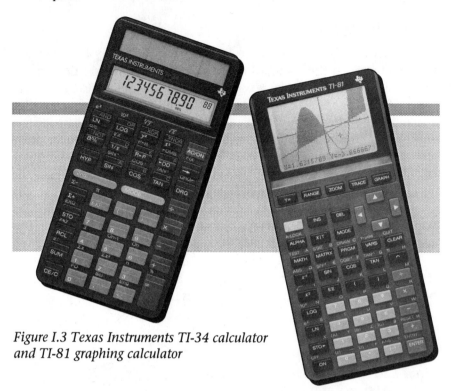

Figure I.3 Texas Instruments TI-34 calculator and TI-81 graphing calculator

Graphing

More so than basic and scientific calculators, those that have graphing capability have the power to significantly change the way secondary and post-secondary mathematics are taught. These calculators are so powerful that even the most traditional of secondary mathematics teachers get excited with the potential of graphing calculators. They add a visual dimension to the teaching of mathematics with the ability to graph functions. In addition to a full range of graphing functions, these calculators also have the features of a standard scientific calculator, and statistical and matrix math capability. The most popular of the graphing calculators is the Texas Instruments TI-81.

One of the tenets of this book is that technology is constantly changing and that mathematics teachers must use this changing technology to more effectively teach mathematics. A new round of graphing calculators are now being produced that are even more powerful than the first generation of graphing calculators. An example of one of

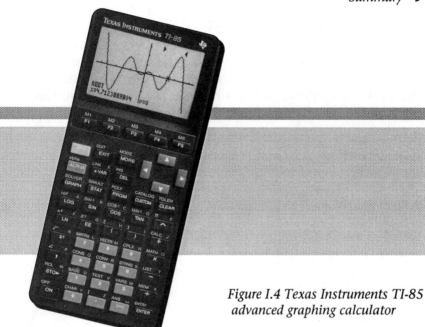

*Figure I.4 Texas Instruments TI-85
advanced graphing calculator*

these graphing calculators is the Texas Instruments TI-85, which has even more graphing power and equation-solving capability than the TI-81.

As prices for graphing calculators continue to decrease, more and more high schools will be able to offer graphics-enhanced courses for their students. Their use need not be restricted to calculus and pre-calculus. Their use has the potential to dramatically change the way basic algebra concepts are taught.

Though I have "favorite activities" for use with graphing calculators, they are not in this book. All of the activities in this book can be used with any calculator-even a graphing calculator. But the graphing calculator is so specialized that there are no activities in this book specific to them. The use of calculators like the Math Explorer used at the middle school level and graphing calculators used at the secondary level enable teachers to move closer to the vision of mathematics education as described in the NCTM Standards.

SUMMARY

The purpose of the material in this initial chapter was to provide background information on the use of calculators in classrooms and to give teachers a preview of the book so it can be used more effectively.

As you read through the chapters, pick and choose those activities which you can use with your students. Revise and extend the activities as you teach mathematics to your students. This book will help you integrate calculator usage into your mathematics program and provide your students with rich investigations in mathematics. Read on!

CHAPTER II

"Showstoppers"

INTRODUCTION

This chapter of "Favorite Calculator Lessons" contains seven different activities. As will be repeated several times, these activities are more than single-period lessons-with extensions and additional explorations, they become full, rich investigations. I like to use the term "showstoppers" to describe them because they are highly motivational and can ignite that spark we all desire in our classrooms. Each of the activities could have been placed in other chapters of this book but they deserve their own chapter.

Another characteristic all these activity-investigations share is that they involve the use of the calculator. Regardless of the kind and sophistication of the calculators you use with your students, every one of these activities can be used. These activities truly exemplify various ways calculators can be integrated into the teaching and learning of mathematics.

As with all lessons in this book, it is assumed that all students have access to calculators at all times. As you go through the lesson scripts in this chapter and other chapters, you will see that there is nothing to fear about "total access" to calculators. Their use is interwoven with the mathematics. If you develop the attitude toward calculator use suggested by this book, you will become confident in your ability to use calculators to effectively teach mathematics.

All of these activities require participation-both by your students and you. With the exception of distributing a sheet of number grids for one of the activities, none of them require "purple-inking" your students. This is a reference to the distribution of worksheet after worksheet after worksheet to your students-a common occurrence, sad to say, in many mathematics classrooms. Worksheets are useful and necessary in a mathematics classroom but if you follow the scripts for these lessons, you will have successful lessons which are not dependent on many handouts.

With the exception of one activity specific to primary mathematics, the others can be used from upper elementary through high school mathematics. Algebraic rationales accompany most of the activities which provide you with extensions for high school students.

Whether or not you use calculators on a regular basis with your students, if you get excited as you read the lesson narratives, then you will be hooked. Read on!

MAGIC ADDITION AND THE SWAMI

Prologue

I wish I could give credit to someone for this activity. But I cannot. It has been around for a long time. It is what might be referred to as a generic activity. It is included in many books on motivational activities; I used it in the classroom in pre-calculator days and continue to use it now to start my calculator workshops. It is included in this book on teaching with calculators for a reason which will become apparent. For now, assume that all students have a calculator on their desks.

Use props to enliven a classroom presentation. You can ham it up here and wear the clothes of a swami. Years ago, I walked into my classroom with a turban, made by my wife, on my head. I had a cloak draped over my shoulders; the cloak was an ornate tablecover I brought back from a trip to Spain. Needless to say, I had the attention of my students.

Procedure

Whether or not you use a turban, announce to the class that you are going to perform magic today. On the chalkboard or overhead projector, write a column of numbers from 1 to 10. Ask for a single-digit number. Does it have to be a single-digit number? No, but it will make your job easier. A student gives you "8." Write the "8" next to the "1." Ask for a second number. Suppose you are given "5." Write the "5" next to the "2" in the list. (See figure II.1.)

Once you have two numbers, you are ready to proceed. Ask the class for the sum of 5 and 8 (13). Write the "13" next to the "3" in the list. The fourth number will be the sum of the second and third numbers (5 + 13 = 18), the fifth number, the sum of the third and fourth numbers

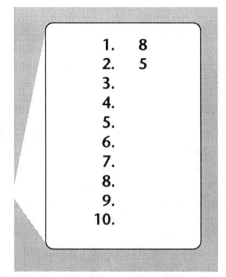

Figure II.1

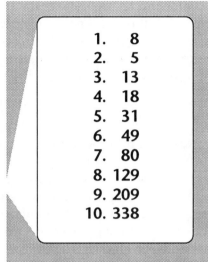

Figure II.2

(13 + 18 = 31), and so on. Continue until you have ten numbers. (See Figure II.2.)

Now tell your students to find the sum of the ten numbers that were just generated. As the students are about to begin, quickly write the sum-which you already know is "880"-on the blackboard without letting the students see the sum. Announce that you already have written the sum on the blackboard. After most students have found the sum of the ten numbers, call on one of them to give the sum. One will declare "880." You ceremoniously uncover the same sum, "880."

Review how the numbers were generated. Now have students make their own columns of numbers from 1 to 10 and pick their own two starting numbers. Each generates a set of ten numbers and finds the sum of the ten numbers. Tell them that when they have found their sums to raise their hands. Tell them not to let you see their sum but just their list of numbers and within seconds, you will tell them their sum.

At this point, roam around the room theatrically "divining" answers. Students will be convinced that you possess some form of magic. They will make list after list to try to trip you up. As long as you can do mental math, you will be successful as you declare each student's sum. The "trick?" The sum will always be 11 x the seventh number. But do not tell students! The object of the lesson is to have them explore and try to discover the pattern. At most, give them this one hint. "What operation is a quick way of repeating addition?" Someone will say "multiplication." That's it-don't say anything else except words of support and encouragement. Students will spend the class period searching for why the "trick" works-and that is what you want.

Follow-Up

Notice at no time did the above lesson script suggest a statement such as "Now use your calculators to find the sum of the ten numbers." It is obvious to use a calculator to add ten 2, 3, and 4-digit numbers. This is an example of an activity that integrates the calculator into a mathematics lesson. It is appropriate to use calculators here. The use of the calculator permits students to concentrate on pattern searches and not get bogged down with the computations. If students have access to calculators at all times, you, as teacher, have nothing to fear. In this case, they are available and will be used when necessary. Teaching students to use calculators appropriately is an important part of teaching mathematics. But the lesson is far from over. You start with a pattern involving arithmetic and extend it to a problem-solving lesson involving a pattern search.

At the middle school level, some students, given the above hint, will try dividing the sum by some of the numbers until they find a "guzinta." Now don't tell me you don't know what a "guzinta" is; 3 "guzinta" 12 four times. In other words, students will explore to see if one or more of the numbers in the list is a factor of the sum. When the sum is divided by the seventh number, the quotient will be 11. Doing the same for several other lists, the same relationship holds; the sum is always 11 x the seventh number. That is what exploring with a calculator is all about.

For students who have some algebra skills, provide an algebraic proof of the pattern. Using variables a and b for the two starting numbers, have students help you find algebraic representations of each of the numbers. "What is the algebraic representation of the third number?" (a + b), etc. Combine the ten numbers for a sum of 55a + 88b. (See Figure II.3.) In factored form, the sum is 11 x (5a + 8b); the algebraic representation of the seventh number is 5a + 8b. So, there it is in algebraic form; the sum is 11 x the seventh number.

This lesson, which may span more than the traditional forty-five or sixty-minute period, has it all. You start with an arithmetic pattern,

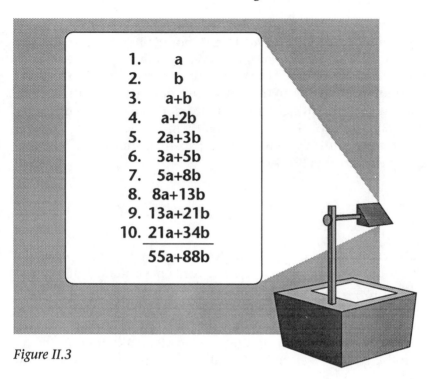

1. a
2. b
3. a+b
4. a+2b
5. 2a+3b
6. 3a+5b
7. 5a+8b
8. 8a+13b
9. 13a+21b
10. 21a+34b

    55a+88b

Figure II.3

integrate the use of the calculator, and end up with an algebraic proof of the arithmetic pattern. You can also bring in some history of mathematics here since this is a Fibonacci sequence where each number after the first two are sums of the previous two numbers. One of the goals of mathematics education is to help students see connections in mathematics. This activity and others like it help students see the intertwining of the arithmetic and algebra strands.

When in the classroom, I started off the year with this activity; this was my first lesson. Students would leave that first class saying "this class is going to be fun" and "he made us think today." You can distribute books, make group assignments, have students fill out all the necessary forms on the second day. Do an activity like this one on the first day. It will set the tone for the rest of the year.

To close this chapter, let me tell you about Vincent's discovery. Vincent was a student in one of my seventh grade classes many years ago. I did the Swami bit and had this class hooked. They tried everything to wrest the explanation from me but I was adamant. "Keep working on it." Vincent was the kind of student we wish filled each of our classes. He tried many hunches and weeks later, entered the room with a triumphant smile on his face. "I got it," he announced. "The answer will always be ten times the seventh number plus the seventh number." Is that beautiful? Of course, that is the same as 11 x the seventh number, according to the distributive property of multiplication over addition. Vincent's classmates were impressed with his discovery and I was impressed with his tenacity. He made me see that I was on the right track in the way I was teaching mathematics and demanding that students learn to think.

7, 11, AND 13

Prologue

This activity should be a part of every mathematics teacher's bag of tricks. It can be used anytime after students have studied division of whole numbers. I used it when teaching prime factorizations of numbers. Students at the middle school level are capable of explaining the pattern using the mathematics they have learned thus far; those with algebra skills can follow an algebraic explanation. As with other activities in this book, it is assumed that all students in the class have calculators.

Procedure

As you provide directions to students, work through a problem on the chalkboard or overhead projector. The popular overhead calculators are excellent for this purpose. Give the directions orally and work through an example at the same time.

	Example
1. "Key in a three-digit number."	629
2. "Key in the same three digits; you now have a 6-digit number in your display."	629629
3. "Press $\div$ 7 $=$."	89947
4. "Press $\div$ 11 $=$."	8177
5. "Press $\div$ 13 $=$."	629

Students will be surprised to see that following the procedure results in the original display. Make sure students understand the directions. Challenge them to try different three-digit numbers to see if the pattern holds. Have them try changing the order of the three divisors to see if the change in order affects the result. Students will try many different instances; the result will always be the same. Questions will be asked. "Can I use the same digits for my three-digit number?" Tell them to test their questions-offer encouragement but do not give them a yes or no answer. What you want them to discover is why you always end up with the original three-digit number.

Sooner or later, students will multiply 7 by 11 by 13. The product of these three numbers is 1,001. They then will multiply a three-digit number by 1,001; the product will be a six-digit number, with the three digits repeating. Whether they can verbalize things at this point, the rationale for the pattern has been found. The six-digit number is the same as 1,001 x the three-digit number and the prime factorization of 1,001 is 7 x 11 x 13.

Here is an algebraic proof:

1. Start with a three-digit number using a, b, and c, $a \neq 0$
   abc
2. Repeat the digits for a six-digit number
   abcabc =
3. Expand the six-digit number,
   $a \cdot 10^5 + b \cdot 10^4 + c \cdot 10^3 + a \cdot 10^2 + b \cdot 10^1 + c \cdot 1 =$
4. Rearrange terms,
   $a \cdot 10^5 + a \cdot 10^2 + b \cdot 10^4 + b \cdot 10^1 + c \cdot 10^3 + c \cdot 1 =$
5. Factor,
   $a \cdot 10^2 \cdot (10^3 + 1) + b \cdot 10^1 \cdot (10^3 + 1) + c \cdot (10^3 + 1) =$
6. Now factor out $10^3 + 1$,
   $(10^3 + 1) \cdot (a \cdot 10^2 + b \cdot 10^1 + c) =$
7. In standard form,
   $1,001 \cdot abc =$
8. In factored form,
   $7 \cdot 11 \cdot 13 \cdot abc$

Follow-Up

It is not hard to see how the use of the calculator aids the problem-solving process with this activity. Years ago, I used this activity in pre-calculator classrooms. No matter how proficient students were with the long division paper and pencil algorithm, they would get so bogged down with the computations that any possibility of exploring patterns and searching for a rationale were lost. This is one of the most popular activities in my teacher workshops. Teachers can see the obvious advantages for using calculators. Again, calculator use was integrated into an exploration of an arithmetic pattern leading to a rationale for the pattern. And once again, the emphasis is on student thinking.

1992 AND OTHER DATES

Prologue

In this activity students follow your directions and find the sum of five numbers selected from a grid of 25 numbers. Regardless of the five numbers they choose, all get the same sum. This lesson has never failed the author in getting students excited about mathematics. Once you understand the technique for creating grids like the ones used in this activity, you can use the technique several times during the year. An extension will suggest integrating this mathematics lesson with dates in history. Again, as with other lessons in this chapter, the calculator is integrated into the lesson in a manner as innocuous as the use of a pencil, compass, or protractor. If this lesson is understood and used by the teacher, then he/she will be successful in integrating calculators into mathematics instruction.

Use this activity as a problem-solving lesson at the middle school level. Using two-digit numbers, the lesson can be used in the elementary grades. With a suggested extension, you have an effective algebra lesson. For now, assume students have calculators on their desks.

Procedure

Prepare a student handout with several copies of figure II.4 and several blank grids which will be used later to show a rationale for the technique.

Students must understand the directions you will give to them orally. For the 5 x 5 grid, there are 25 three-digit numbers. Working with one of the grids, give the following directions:

1. "Circle any one of the three-digit numbers in the grid."
2. "Now after circling the number, cross out all other numbers that are in the same row and column as the number you circled."
3. "Circle a second number that has not been circled or crossed out."

458	423	516	440	430
419	384	477	401	391
342	307	400	324	314
411	376	469	393	383
385	350	443	367	357

Figure II.4

458	423	516	440	430
419	384	477	401	391
342	307	400	324	314
411	376	469	393	383
385	350	443	367	357

Figure II.5

4. "Now after circling the second number, cross out all other numbers that are in the same row and column as the number you circled."
5. "Circle a third number that has not been circled or crossed out."
6. "Now after circling the third number, cross out all other numbers that are in the same row and column as the number you circled."
7. "Circle a fourth number, then cross out all other numbers that are in the same row and column as the number you circled."
8. "There should be one number left that has not been circled or crossed out. Is that correct? Circle this last number."
9. "You now have five circled numbers. (An example of a completed grid is shown in figure II.5.) Find the sum of the five circled numbers."

Students started with different "first" numbers and are fascinated when each of them has the same sum for their five circled numbers, 1992. Have them use the other grids to go through the process again beginning with different starting numbers. If the above directions are followed each time, the sum will always be the same, 1992. What you want students to discover is "How come?"

Closure to this lesson may not come at the end of a standard class period. You want students to explore, to at least determine what following the directions will guarantee. Some students will determine that for the "trick" to work, there must be only one number on each

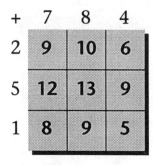

Figure II.6

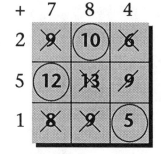

Figure II.7

row and column. Failure to follow the directions will result in having two numbers on a row or column and the sum will not be 1992. Other students will discover that the differences between corresponding numbers in different columns will be constant; e.g., in figure II.4, the corresponding numbers in the first two columns have the same difference of 35; 458 - 423 = 35, 419 - 384 = 35, etc. This suggests an explanation for the pattern. What you want to do at this point is to use the strategy of starting with a simpler problem to show why the sum will always be the same regardless of what starting number is chosen.

What you have here is nothing more complex than an addition table! What the student does not see are the ten row and column headings that were used to generate the 25 numbers in the addition table. Still don't see, do you? Let's work with a simpler problem and make a 3 x 3 addition table. Take six numbers; e.g., 2, 5, 1, 7, 8, and 4. The sum of these six numbers is 27. Now use the six numbers to make an addition table. By adding numbers in rows and columns, the nine numbers in figure II.6 are generated.

This is how the grid in figure II.4 was made, but you did not see the numbers that were used to generate the 25 numbers. Now pick a number in the grid; e.g., 12 and circle it. What does the 12 represent? It is the sum of 7 and 5; by crossing out the other numbers in the same row and column as 12, you guarantee that the numbers 7 and 5 from the six column and row headings will not be used again. Let's circle 5 in the grid; that is the sum of 4 and 1; by crossing out the other numbers in the same row and column as the 5, you have guaranteed that the 4 and 1 will not be used again in the final sum. Since we are working with a 3 x 3 grid, there is only one number left that has not been crossed out or circled. If it is circled (see figure II.7) and we find the sum of the three circled numbers, 12, 5, and 10, the sum will be the same as the sum of the six numbers we started with, 27. Guaranteed!

Students can follow the above explanation and are able to generalize to a 4 x 4, 5 x 5, or n x n grid. Once students understand how the grid was developed, they will want to know what ten numbers were used for a sum of 1992. Turn that into another project and see if your students can figure out the ten numbers.

Let's assume it is 1993 and this is the first time you are reading this book and would like to use this activity. Obviously, you want the final sum of the five circled numbers to be 1993, not 1992. The activity is still valid–you have to make a minor revision with the numbers. In workshops, I use this as an additional problem-solving activity. Even without knowing the ten numbers with a sum of 1992 that were used for the row and column headings, how many of them would need to be changed for a sum of 1993? Only one of them, 1993 = 1992 + 1. But once a row or column is increased by 1, how many numbers in the grid are affected? Five row or column numbers are affected and each must be increased by 1. Refer to figure II.4. Let's assume the number in the first column will need to be increased by 1; 458 to 459, 419 to 420, 342 to 343, 411 to 412, and 385 to 386. With these changes, the grid is now valid for the year 1993. You can change it for 1994, 1995, ...

Another extension is to have groups of students create grids with sums that are famous dates in history; e.g., 1492, 1776, and 1812. How do you do that? It is easy. For example, start with the date that Columbus discovered America, 1492. For a 5 x 5 grid, you need ten numbers. Pick a number (245) and subtract it from 1,492; 1,492 - 245 = 1,247. Pick another number (176) and subtract it from 1,247; 1,247 - 176 = 1,071. Keep going until you have ten numbers and have "used up" the desired sum, 1,492. Here is a neat technique that will simplify your work-and use technology! Use the memory keys; key in: 1492 [M+] 245 [M-] [MRC] 176 [M-] [MRC] etc. The [MRC] key is used to keep track of the remainders. Use the ten numbers to create an addition table with the ten numbers placed in the row and column headings. Add row by column headings and you generate a 5 x 5 table. Erase the column and row headings and you have a grid with a sum of 1492, providing, of course, that the directions are followed (see figure II.8 for the grid with row and column headings intact). Use in October!

Use variables and turn the activity into an algebra lesson. A grid with variables is shown in figure II.9.

+	245	176	84	63	204
91	336	267	175	154	295
267	512	443	351	330	471
73	318	249	157	136	277
127	372	303	201	190	331
162	407	338	246	225	366

When did Columbus discover America?

Figure II.8

+	f	g	h	i	j
a	a + f	a + g	a + h	a + i	a + j
b	b + f	b + g	b + h	b + i	b + j
c	c + f	c + g	c + h	c + i	c + j
d	d + f	d + g	d + h	d + i	d + j
e	e + f	e + g	e + h	e + i	e + j

Figure II.9

The algebraic sums of row and column headings are shown in the grid. In figure II.10, five terms are circled; the algebraic sum of these ten terms is the same as the sum of the ten variables, $a + b + c + d + e + f + g + h + i + j$.

With the fraction capability of the Texas Instruments TI-12 Math Explorer, grids with fractions can be explored. Figure II.11 is an example of a 3 x 3 fraction grid with a sum of 2 13/40.

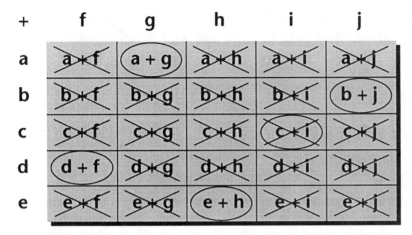

Figure II.10

+	$\frac{1}{4}$	$\frac{2}{5}$	$\frac{3}{8}$
$\frac{1}{2}$	$\frac{3}{4}$	$\frac{9}{20}$	$\frac{7}{8}$
$\frac{3}{5}$	$\frac{17}{20}$	1	$\frac{39}{40}$
$\frac{1}{5}$	$\frac{9}{20}$	$\frac{3}{5}$	$\frac{23}{40}$

Fraction grid with a sum of $2\frac{13}{40}$

Figure II.11

Follow-Up

At no time in the above lesson script is the word "calculator" used and yet it is an excellent lesson for integrating calculator use. It is appropriate to use calculators to find sums of 5 three-digit numbers; it is not necessary to direct students to use their calculators. If you follow the suggested script, students will naturally use their calculators to find the sum of the numbers. Further, the exploring and testing of hunches in attempts to determine "how come?" is simplified with calculator use. This activity demonstrates the ease of integrating calculators into mathematics instruction. This lesson includes problem solving, communication, exploration, and use of higher-order thinking skills-all facilitated with the use of calculators.

WHAT'S THE PATTERN?

Prologue

Here is an activity which involves a pattern search facilitated by the use of calculators. Some teachers may be aware of a specific case of the pattern but are unaware of the more general case. This activity can be used after students have worked with multiplication of two-digit numbers. It is an excellent activity to use with algebra students to show the intertwining of the strands of arithmetic and algebra.

Procedure

Explain to students that you are going to give them a set of multiplications and they have to determine the products as quickly as possible. "At some point, many of you will see something and be able to do the computations mentally. Don't tell us what you see; just call out the product."

Start with 25 x 25. The first part of this activity involves multiplying a number by itself or squaring a number. If basic calculators are being used, students will key in n$\boxed{\times}$ n$\boxed{=}$ or n$\boxed{\times}$ $\boxed{=}$ (using the constant feature). If the TI-12 Math Explorer or scientific calculator is being used, students can key in n$\boxed{x^2}$.

Write the computations on the overhead or blackboard:

25 x 25	Response: "625"
45 x 45	Response: "2025"
35 x 35	Response: "1225"
75 x 75	Response: "5625"
55 x 55	Response: "3025"

By now, some students have a hunch. If not, tell students to examine each product listed and look at the number being multiplied. By not separating the products into periods using commas, you have provided a visual clue for students. Continue:

65 x 65 One of your students yells out "4225." The student is correct; the rest of the class looks at the student and wonders from what planet this student is from.

95 x 95 A volunteer calls out, "9025." More students begin to see something. Again:

85 x 85 Several of the students' hands are now up. "7225." "Try this one."

105 x 105 One or two students will call out, "11025." Now you got them. "Try this one."

115 x 115 A few students will respond, "13225."

Half the class is doing the multiplications mentally. The other half might well be checking the products using their calculators. All students are looking for a pattern.

Now announce that you are going to make a slight change, and for those students who have been doing the multiplications mentally to continue doing whatever they have been doing.

24 x 26	Response: "624"
37 x 33	Response: "1221"
52 x 58	Response: "3016"
61 x 69	Response: "4209"
34 x 36	Response: "1224"
93 x 97	Response: "9021"
72 x 78	Response: "5616"

By now, more students have joined the mental-math group and are telling you "give us another." Continue:

48 x 42	Response: "2016"
67 x 63	Response: "4221"
81 x 89	Response: "7209"

Can the reader explain what's happening? By now, students are pleading with you to let them explain the pattern. Do not accept an explanation yet. It is time to "break a few bubbles." "Try this one."

46 x 43 Response: "2018" You declare, "No, whatever you are doing, it will not work for this one." Obviously, there is a product for this multiplication, but it is not 2018. Students will refine their thinking. Now give them this one:

54 x 66 Response: "It won't work for that one." This response is correct. Now you are ready to have a student explain the pattern and the criteria for using it. A typical response is:

If the tens' digits of the numbers being multiplied are the same and the sum of the units' digits is 10, then you multiply the tens' digit by the next larger digit and multiply the units' digits by each other and put it all together."

Show an example. For 38 x 32, 3 x 4 = 12; 8 x 2 = 16; answer: 1216

Provide additional computations for students to use the pattern.

You now have an opportunity to connect the strands of arithmetic and algebra by providing an algebraic proof.

a, b, c, {1, 2, 3, ..., 9} and b + c = 10

The two-digit numbers have the form 10a + b and 10a + c where b + c = 10

$$
\begin{aligned}
(10a + b)(10a + c) &= 10a \cdot 10a + 10ac + 10ab + bc \\
&= 100a^2 + 10a(b + c) + bc \\
&= 100a^2 + 10a \cdot 10 + bc \\
&= 100a^2 + 100a + bc \\
&= 100a(a + 1) + bc
\end{aligned}
$$

There it is; the tens' digit is multiplied by the next consecutive digit then multiplied by 100 and the units' digits are multiplied together.

Follow-Up

This activity has been included in this chapter to illustrate an example of the transition to calculator-integrated instruction. The focus of this activity is on discovering a pattern. Access to calculators does not detract from this goal; in fact, it aids the process. Students need to be involved in activities which promote searching for patterns in mathematics. Activities such as this one get students thinking about why numbers and operations behave the way they do.

PROBLEM-SOLVING WITH "LITTLE NUMBERS" OR EXPONENTS

Prologue

This activity could be placed in just about any of the chapters in this book. It involves the problem solving strategy of "guess-and-check;" after students learn the generalization involved, they are engaged in a neat problem-solving activity in finding solutions to equations in an informal approach. But since estimation skills are used in this activity, it could be placed in the estimation chapter. Mental math is used so it could also be placed in the chapter on mental math. The same could be said for placing this activity in the chapter on patterns or in the chapter on number crunching. It is included in this chapter because it involves all of the above topics and is truly a "show stopper."

As with other investigations in this chapter, this activity may take several class periods to complete. It can be used with elementary students and with high school students. I once taught the lesson to gifted third graders; I used the term "little numbers" instead of "exponents" and it worked well. It will be described here as if it was being used with elementary students who have worked with multiplication of whole numbers.

This investigation utilizes the operation of multiplication and the constant capability of a basic calculator such as the Texas Instruments TI-108 calculator. The constant feature explained here will also work on the Texas Instruments TI-12, Math Explorer, even though the Math Explorer has a separate constant key for repeated calculations using the same number.

The description below assumes that students are familiar with the constant feature of a basic calculator. For multiplication, if 3 $\boxed{\times}$ 4 $\boxed{=}$ is pressed, the display reads "12." Now press 5 $\boxed{=}$. The display reads "15." Press 2 $\boxed{=}$ for a display of "6." Press 9 $\boxed{=}$. The display reads "27." Do you see what is happening? In the absence of a second factor, the calculator uses the first factor from the original multiplication (3) and multiplies it by the number in the display. This feature enables the user to use a shortcut when using the same number as a factor repeatedly.

Procedure

Use the chalkboard or overhead projector to give students the following sets of sequences. Students are to key in sequences and generalize their answers. Have students call out the products as quickly as you can write them.

2 $\boxed{\times}$ $\boxed{=}$	Response: "Four."
3 $\boxed{\times}$ $\boxed{=}$	Response: "Nine."
5 $\boxed{\times}$ $\boxed{=}$	Response: "Twenty-five."
8 $\boxed{\times}$ $\boxed{=}$	Response: "Sixty-four."

(By now, many students are calling out answers using mental math.)

6 [x] [=]   Response: "Thirty-six."
4 [x] [=]   Response: "Sixteen."
9 [x] [=]   Response: "Eighty-one."

Now have a student generalize the products. Ask what is happening here. A typical response from elementary students is "The number is being multiplied by itself." Or "The number is used in multiplication two times." Middle school students may give a geometric interpretation, "You're squaring the numbers."

So, 2 [x] [=] is a calculator shortcut for 2 x 2.

Continue. Try to keep all these sets of sequences on the chalkboard or on one overhead projectual so students will be able to generalize a pattern when you are ready.

2 [x] [=] [=]   Response: "Eight."
3 [x] [=] [=]   Response: "Twenty-seven."
5 [x] [=] [=]   Response: "One hundred, twenty-five."
6 [x] [=] [=]   Response: "Two hundred, sixteen."
4 [x] [=] [=]   Response: "Sixty-four."
9 [x] [=] [=]   Response: "Seven hundred, twenty-nine."

What is happening this time? "The number is being used in multiplication three times." Middle school students say, "You're cubing the numbers."

So, 2 [x] [=] [=] is a calculator shortcut for 2 x 2 x 2. This can all be done without use of the word "factor" but if it is part of the students' vocabulary, then by all means, use the word. At this point, tell the class that math teachers are lazy and rather than use 2 x 2 x 2 to show three factors of two, you are going to use a "little three" to show three factors of two, as in 2^3. "What does 5^3 mean?" (Three factors of 5) Make sure they understand the "little number" device.

Let's do it one more time:

2 [x] [=] [=] [=]   Response: "Sixteen."
3 [x] [=] [=] [=]   Response: "Eighty-one."
4 [x] [=] [=] [=]   Response: "Two hundred, fifty-six."
5 [x] [=] [=] [=]   Response: "Six hundred, twenty-five."

Have a student generalize. "The number is being used in multiplication four times."

So, 2 [x] [=] [=] [=] is a calculator shortcut for 2 x 2 x 2 x 2 or 2^4.

Now you want to put it all together. "When the product is the result of using four factors, how many $=$ keys were used?" An alternate question to ask is "When the "little number" is a "4" how many $=$ keys are used?" Students will respond with "Three." "When the product is the result of using three factors, how many $=$ keys were used?" Students will respond with "Two." "When the product is the result of using two factors or the "little number" is a "2", how many $=$ keys were used?" Students will respond with "One." Now ask what shortcut would you use to find: 4 x 4 x 4 x 4 x 4 x 4 or 4^6? Students will answer before calculating, "Do $4\boxed{\times}\boxed{=}\boxed{=}\boxed{=}\boxed{=}\boxed{=}$."

Once students understand the generalization that the number of $=$ keys used will be one less than the number of factors or the "little number," provide practice in using the generalization:

2^8	Answer: 256
7^3	Answer: 343
3^7	Answer: 6,561
4^4	Answer: 256
13^3	Answer: 2,197
24^2	Answer: 576
9^5	Answer: 59,049
2^{10}	Answer: 1,024

Everyone needs to be able to use the shortcut before going on to the problem-solving activity which is dependent on the use of the shortcut. There are many sidetrips that can be taken at this point. For instance, ask students why 2^8 and 4^4 yield the same product. How about 4^3 and 8^2; do they yield the same product? You could lead into a discussion of the prime factorization of numbers showing that the above pairs of exponential expressions have the same prime factorizations.

Another sidetrip involves using the shortcut to investigate unit digits of products of the same number raised to different powers. For example, (most of these will be done mentally by students):

$2^1 = 2$	Unit digit of product: 2
$2^2 = 4$	Unit digit of product: 4
$2^3 = 8$	Unit digit of product: 8
$2^4 = 16$	Unit digit of product: 6
$2^5 = 32$	Unit digit of product: 2
$2^6 = 64$	Unit digit of product: 4
$2^7 = 128$	Unit digit of product: 8
$2^8 = 256$	Unit digit of product: 6

Notice the repeating pattern of the unit digits. Have students generalize to any number with a unit digit of 2 raised to a power. "The product will always end in a 2, 4, 8, or 6." For example, what is the unit digit of 32^3? (8, $32^3 = 32,768$) Similar investigations with numbers that end in a 1, 3, 4, 5, etc. raised to various patterns will yield other patterns.

Both of the above sidetrips provide excellent opportunities for student journal writing. Whether the sidetrips are taken, let us now involve students in a problem-solving experience. Put this equation on the chalkboard or overhead:

$\square^4 = 2,401$. "What number goes in the box?"

Students are going to respond, "What do we do?" Remind them that they learned a generalization and that they should use it. Students usually do not need any more hints. At this level they have no algebra skills to use to solve these equations. Solving the equations in the manner suggested provides effective pre-algebra skill development. Using a combination of the generalization, number sense, estimation skills, and mental math, a student will triumphantly call out, "Seven." Have all students check the student's work by pressing

$7 \boxed{\times} \boxed{=} \boxed{=} \boxed{=}$. The display will read 2,401.

You want students to use one of the most effective problem-solving strategies that is used in real-world applications-guess and check. Students try a number, use the generalization and if the target number is not reached, then the guess is adjusted up or down and a new number tried. Continue:

$\square^3 = 2,197$	Answer: 13
$\square^2 = 1,681$	Answer: 41
$\square^5 = 1,024$	Answer: 4
$\square^5 = 248,832$	Answer: 12
$\square^4 = 279,841$	Answer: 23
$\square^8 = 1,679,616$	Answer: 6

Students will be calling out, "Give us another." Provide additional examples. As the provider of the examples, you have to work quickly. For example, press $8 \boxed{\times} \boxed{=} \boxed{=} \boxed{=} \boxed{=} \boxed{=}$. You will get a display of 262,144. Write on the chalkboard " $\square^6 = 262,144$ and remember your base number, 8.

The final step in this activity or set of activities is to have the students become the example providers. Check each volunteer 's work before he/she puts the example on the chalkboard.

Follow-Up

The above procedure describes an activity which, if the sidetrips are taken, can be developed into a week-long unit of work. By effective use of the chalkboard or overhead, no worksheets are involved—a worthy goal in itself. Students are involved in investigations in which they explore patterns, use problem solving, estimation, and mental-math skills. Much of the above can be accomplished using a cooperative learning setup. For example, when doing the sidetrip involving unit digits, use cooperative groups and have each group report on its findings. This is another of those activities that has it all and that is why it is "one of my favorite things."

PLAY IT AGAIN...AND AGAIN

Prologue

This activity is appropriate for primary students. It can be used as a multi-day investigation or as several separate lessons. It utilizes the constant capability of basic calculators like the Texas Instruments TI-108 and the TI MathMate.

This activity should be used by those who see no role for the calculator in the primary grades, believing that the use of calculators will deter students learning basic computational skills. Every time I have used this activity with first and second graders I am amazed at their use of number sense and their eagerness to explore patterns.

Procedure

The first part of this investigation involves teaching the constant capability of the calculator to do repeated addition and subtraction. Both calculators mentioned above have corresponding overhead models which can be used in a demonstration mode as you introduce the lesson. With a blank transparency placed under the Overhead™ Calculator, you can key in sequences and write them on the transparency for students to see.

Give the following directions:

"Press 2 $+$ 3 $=$ "	"What number is in your display."	(5)
"Now press 4 $=$ "	"What number is in your display."	(7)
"Press 1 $=$ "	"What number is in your display."	(4)
"Press 6 $=$ "	"What number is in your display."	(9)

"Press 7 $=$ "   "What number is in your display." (10)
"Press 5 $=$ "   "What number is in your display." (8)

"Can anyone explain what is happening?"

If no one can explain the above pattern of displays, try several other similar sets of sequences. In the absence of a second addend and operation, the calculator "remembers" the second addend (3) of the original addition problem and adds it to each of the subsequent numbers that are entered.

    First display: 5   2 + 3
    Next display: 7   4 + 3
    Next display: 4   1 + 3
    Next display: 9   6 + 3
    Next display: 10   7 + 3
    Next display: 8   5 + 3

Practice adding 2 to several numbers:

    5 $+$ 2 $=$ 4 $=$ 7 $=$ 1 $=$ 8 $=$

Respective displays are:

    7, 6, 9, 3, and 10

Practice adding 5 to several numbers:

    3 $+$ 5 $=$ 7 $=$ 2 $=$ 10 $=$ 13 $=$

Respective displays are:

    8, 12, 7, 15, and 18

Do additional sequences till all students understand that the second addend from the original addition problem is used repeatedly as a constant.

Now show students how to count by 2's starting at 0:

    Press: 0 $+$ 2 $=$ $=$ $=$ $=$ $=$ $=$ $=$ etc.

Each time the $=$ key is pressed, the display will read 2, 4, 6, 8, 10, 12, 14, etc.

Count by 3's starting at 0:

    Press: 0 $+$ 3 $=$ $=$ $=$ $=$ $=$ $=$ $=$ etc.

Each time the $=$ key is pressed, the display will read 3, 6, 9, 12, 15, 18, 21, etc.

These sequences will also generate the same displays using the TI MathMate:

2⊕⊜⊜⊜⊜⊜⊜⊜etc.
3⊕⊜⊜⊜⊜⊜⊜⊜etc.

These sequences also work on the TI-108 as long as the display is cleared after each set of sequences.

Now show students how to count by 2's starting at a non-zero number, e.g., 1:

Press: 1⊕2⊜⊜⊜⊜⊜⊜⊜etc.

Each time the ⊜ key is pressed, the display will read 3, 5, 7, 9, 11, 13, 15, etc.

Count by 3's starting at 4:

Press: 4⊕3⊜⊜⊜⊜⊜⊜⊜etc.

Each time the ⊜ key is pressed, the display will read 7, 10, 13, 16, 19, 22, 25, etc.

At this point, the sky is the limit! Have students count by 5's, 10's, etc. The counting and skip counting skills that are taught in the primary grades can be reinforced by using the constant feature of the calculator.

Depending on the ability level of your students and whether you have worked with subtraction, you can either continue on here or jump to the section entitled "Hit the Target."

Let 's look at subtraction.

Give the following directions:

"Press 9⊖3⊜"	"What number is in your display."	(6)
"Now press 4⊜"	"What number is in your display."	(1)
"Press 11⊜"	"What number is in your display."	(8)
"Press 6⊜"	"What number is in your display."	(3)
"Press 17⊜"	"What number is in your display."	(14)
"Press 3⊜"	"What number is in your display."	(0)

"Can anyone explain what is happening?"

If no one can explain what is happening, try several other similar sets of sequences. In the absence of a second number and operation, the calculator "remembers" the second number (3) of the original subtraction problem and subtracts it from each of the subsequent numbers that are entered.

First display: 6   9 - 3
Next display: 1   4 - 3
Next display: 8   11 - 3
Next display: 3   6 - 3
Next display: 14   17 - 3
Next display: 0   3 - 3

Practice subtracting 2 from several numbers:

8 ⊟ 2 ⊜ 4 ⊜ 7 ⊜ 12 ⊜ 2 ⊜

Respective displays are:

6, 2, 5, 10, and 0

Practice subtracting 5 from several numbers:

9 ⊟ 5 ⊜ 7 ⊜ 15 ⊜ 10 ⊜ 5 ⊜

Respective displays are:

4, 2, 10, 5, and 0

Do additional sequences till all students understand that the second number from the original subtraction problem is used repeatedly as a subtraction constant.

Now show students how to count backwards by 1's starting at 20:

Press: 20 ⊟ 1 ⊜ ⊜ ⊜ ⊜ ⊜ ⊜ ⊜ etc.

Each time the ⊜ key is pressed, the display will read 19, 18, 17, 16, 15, 14, 13, etc. Be careful here-your students will keep pressing the ⊜ key and generate negative numbers in the display. This is a fun activity when students call out displays in unison as you press ⊜ keys on the Overhead™ Calculator, "Nineteen, eighteen, seventeen, etc." Take it one step further and have them spell each of the words.

Count backwards by 3's starting at 30:

Press: 30-3 ⊜ ⊜ ⊜ ⊜ ⊜ ⊜ ⊜ ⊜ ⊜ ⊜ etc.

Each time the ⊜ key is pressed, the display will read 27, 24, 21, 18, 15, 12, 9, 6, 3, and 0.

Counting backwards is an important primary skill that can be reinforced by using the constant subtraction feature of the calculator.

You can also use this feature when reinforcing the definition of division as repeated subtraction. 18 ÷ 6 is defined as the number of times 6 can be subtracted from 18. Ask students to key in 18 ⊟ 6 and count the number of ⊟ keys they press to get to 0. Repeat the process with other examples.

Hit the Target

Once students have learned how to use the constant capability of the calculator to do repeated addition and subtraction, play "Hit the Target" with them. You can use the chalkboard, overhead projector, or a large oaktag game board.

Tell students that they have to answer "yes" or "no" before using their calculators.

"Start with 0⊞2. If you keep pressing the ⊟ key, can you reach 10?"

Make sure students understand that they have to "hit" 10 exactly; i.e., they have to get a display of 10. The entire class will respond, "yes." They then key in:

0⊞2⊟⊟⊟⊟ to verify their guess.

"Start with 0⊞5. If you keep pressing the ⊟ key, can you reach 35?" Again, all or most of the class will respond with "yes."

"Start with 0⊞2. If you keep pressing the ⊟ key, can you reach 9?" Most will say "no." They can "hit" 8 and 10, but not 9.

"Start with 1⊞2. If you keep pressing the ⊟ key, can you reach 9?" "Yes."

Use many "easy" ones like the above then try ones like the following:

"Start with 2⊞3. If you keep pressing the ⊟ key, can you reach 17?" ("Yes.")

"Start with 5⊞4. If you keep pressing the ⊟ key, can you reach 25?" ("Yes.")

"Start with 5⊞4. If you keep pressing the ⊟ key, can you reach 38?" ("No.")

"Start with 3⊞10. If you keep pressing the ⊟ key, can you reach 33, 53, 74?"

("Yes, yes, no.")

"Start with 6⊞4. If you keep pressing the ⊟ key, can you reach 22, 33, 46?"

("Yes, no, yes.")

Hit the Target can be played with subtraction, too.

"Start with 20⊟2. If you keep pressing the ⊟ key, can you reach 10?"

('Yes.")

"Start with 20⊟3. If you keep pressing the ⊟ key, can you reach 12?"

('No.")

"Start with 24⊟6. If you keep pressing the ⊟ key, can you reach 0?"

('Yes.")

"Start with 50⊟8. If you keep pressing the ⊟ key, can you reach 18, 10, 3?"

('Yes, yes, no.")

Follow-Up

"Hit the Target" provides an opportunity for exploring on an informal basis concepts like oddness and evenness, multiples, and patterns of units digits when numbers are added and subtracted long before these concepts are engaged in the curriculum. Students will use number-sense skills in this activity.

Once you introduce and play "Hit the Target," your students will want to return to it many times during the year. When initially introduced, use a whole-class approach. When you return to the game, use teams of students, alternating turns, and awarding points. It is simply an excellent primary activity to use when exploring mathematics with calculators.

As was stated in the Prologue, the above teaching of the constant function for addition and subtraction and the game which utilizes repeated addition and subtraction can span several math periods as a multi-day calculator investigation. Or you could teach several one-period lessons spread out over the year, especially if your students have yet to work with the operation of subtraction. Whatever your choice, you will agree that for primary students, "Play It Again...And Again " is a "showstopper!"

A PERCENT EXPLORATION

Prologue

This exploration is in this chapter because it illustrates how a mathematical discovery can be made when least expected. It also suggests that no matter how well planned a lesson is, a sidetrip or response to a question can result in an even more successful lesson. So do not be fearful of scrapping your lesson plan if a "magic moment" seems possible.

In a teacher workshop, a participant reacted to a statement I made and a "minor" discovery was made-at least for me and most of the other participants. Since that experience, I have used the discovery in teaching percent to students and in all my teacher workshops.

The lesson will be described here as it happened in the teacher workshop along with suggestions on how to use it with students.

Procedure

Using a calculator to find a percent of a number depends on the calculator being used. Here's a simple test to determine which of two methods will work on your calculator.

Method 1   Press: 25 %. If the display reads 25, then pressing the % key had no effect on the number in the display. This method works on the Texas Instruments TI-108. To find 25% of 12, key in the base number, 12 first. Press: 12 × 25 %. The display reads 3.

Method 2   Press: 25 %. If the display reads 0.25, then pressing the percent key changes the number in the display (a percent) to a decimal-the number in the display is divided by 100. This is how the % key works on the Texas Instruments scientific calculators and the TI-12 Math Explorer. Finding a percent is analogous to doing it by paper and pencil. Press: 25 % × 12 =. The display reads 3.

Years ago, in a teacher workshop, I was explaining how the % key works on a battery-operated calculator that was similar to the TI-108. As the instruction book recommended, I explained to the participants that you key in the base number first as in method 1 above. One of the teachers raised his hand and said that it was not necessary to key in the base number first, that this sequence will work: 25 × 12 %. Sure enough, the display also reads 3. Quickly juggling some variables mentally, I realized the teacher was right.

In essence, the teacher was saying that 25% of 12 is the same as 12% of 25. In general, a% of b is the same as b% of a. Did you know that? It is easy to show:

Is a% of b = b% of a?

$$a \cdot 1/100 \cdot b = b \cdot 1/100 \cdot a$$
$$a \cdot b \cdot 1/100 = b \cdot a \cdot 1/100$$
$$ab \cdot 1/100 = ba \cdot 1/100$$
$$ab/100 = ab/100$$

Prior to this experience, I cannot remember ever seeing this in any textbook. Since then, I have incorporated this equivalency into any percent unit I have taught. You can use this as a discovery lesson and then as another mental-math technique for students to add to their repertoires.

Use the chalkboard or overhead to provide a set of percent problems for students to compute:

1. 50% of 35   **2.** 35% of 50
3. 60% of 115   **4.** 115% of 60
5. 3% of 87   **6.** 87% of 3
7. 12.5% of 88   **8.** 88% of 12.5

Can you generalize your results?

Another approach is to start a lesson by challenging students with a question like:

"Is 28% of 76 the same as 76% of 28?"

Most students will answer "no" because it "doesn't look right." Notice that if you use numbers that can't be manipulated mentally, there will be more dissenters. Have students try many cases so they become convinced that the formats are equivalent, then prove using variables. Once this is taught, then show students how to use it to compute mentally.

Compute.

1. 44% of 25   (It is easier to find 25% or 1/4 of 44.)
2. 6.8% of 50   (It is easier to find 50% or 1/2 of 6.8)

When providing sets of computation in which students decide an appropriate method to use, include several like the above.

Follow-Up

O.K.-the above is not a major find in mathematics but it illustrates how a lesson can take a sidetrip that can turn into a rewarding experience. The above exploration involves process, number sense, and mental math-all important items to include in a lesson, especially in a classroom where calculators are available to students. Follow up on students' questions—you never know what might happen!

SUMMARY

This chapter contains what I like to refer to as "showstoppers." These activities and investigations are examples of the rich mathematics explorations the NCTM Standards recommend we use to engage our students. All of these activities are highly motivatonal. Only the primary activity depends on a feature of a calculator.They all focus on mathematics and are illustrative of the ease with which calculators can be integrated into the teaching of mathematics.

CHAPTER III

Mental Math

INTRODUCTION

There are activities and investigations in other chapters of this book in which mental-math strategies have been used. But the use of mental math is so important in mathematics education at all levels that the subject is afforded its own chapter. I was tempted to make this the first chapter; the subject matter is that crucial. Quite simply-for many computations the mind is faster than a machine and students must learn to decide the most appropriate method of computation to use.

Many teachers and parents are concerned that students will use calculators for the simplest computations. And do you know what? This happens but can be avoided if you use good techniques in teaching students to use calculators when it is most appropriate and to use mental math when most appropriate. It is your instruction that will determine if students use calculators appropriately. This is the basis for the activities in this chapter.

You can and should use calculators to teach mental mathematics. The trouble is that once you put a "calculator" tag on a lesson or activity, then it is erroneously assumed that you must use a calculator. That's nonsense! A few years from now, when the vision of the Standards is accepted and all students have access to calculators at all times, then there will be no "calculator activities" in textbooks. As in activities and investigations in this book, there will be no instructions to "use your calculator to do the following...." The calculators will be present and used appropriately by students as they learn mathematics.

In the introduction section of the Standards, there is a discussion of deciding on an appropriate computational method to use for various problem situations. If an exact answer is needed, depending on the situation, mental calculation may be warranted. For some simple computations, a paper-and-pencil method might be used. For more complex calculations, a calculator should be used, and for calculations involving iterations, a computer may be the most appropriate method to use.

"LOOK BEFORE YOU LEAP"

Time and time again, I have observed classrooms in which students peck away at their calculators for the simplest of computations. One of the most effective techniques to teach students who have access to calculators in the classroom is one I call "look before you leap." Actually, it is a state of mind. You want students to take a few seconds to decide whether a computation is possible using mental math. At all levels, mental-math strategies are taught consonant with the computational skills which are being taught. Teach these strategies with renewed vigor. With practice, students will use them.

Provide warm-ups, use of flash cards, competitions between individuals and teams, games, and drills to "force" students to use mental math. You want to sensitize them to the need to use mental math. Once they see classmates getting solutions to problems much quicker than they get answers, then they will begin to look for ways to compute faster, i.e., use mental-math strategies.

Effective lessons include a discussion session where students explain how they "attacked" problems. This communication process is an important part of mathematics instruction. Make the term "look before you leap" a part of your vocabulary as you help students use calculators appropriately.

FLASH CARDS

Flash cards are usually thought to be primary oriented, to be used as students are learning basic computational skills. They are still valuable in classrooms where technology is being used and in all grades, not only primary classrooms. I have used flash cards in algebra classes to reinforce computations with integers and manipulative skills with variables and expressions. Students always looked forward to these sessions; they enjoyed the use of flash cards and I was able to do some valuable review.

You want to use flash cards to reinforce basic skills and sensitize students to the use of mental math—remember, "look before you leap."

With third graders who have learned their multiplication facts and have a calculator on their desks, I announce, "Let's review our multi-

23 x 47 + 18

18 + 23 x 47

Figure III.1   *Figure III.2*

plication facts—give me the products of the following numbers as fast as you can." Then I show flash cards with basic multiplication facts—3 x 4, 6 x 1, 5 x 2, etc. These cards can exhibit commutativity, and multiplication by 1 and by 0. Many students will peck away on their calculators but will quickly change their method when other classmates are calling out the products almost instantly as they are shown.

At the middle school level, I will show a card as in figure III.1.

All students will use calculators to find the result, 1099. Now I hit them with the next card which is shown in figure III.2.

Invariably, all or most students will start keying in numbers on their calculators. One or two will call out, "1099—the same as the first one." These students have already learned to "look before you leap." The next time you try a similar pair of flash cards, your students will be ready for you. Use flash cards to review mental-math strategies and use of number properties once a week and students will learn quickly the importance of mental math.

Do not shortchange the use of flash cards at the secondary level. Use them to continue to hone good calculator skills as students study algebra, geometry, and precalculus. For example, the study of special angles has not lost its significance in a classroom in which technology is used. Scientific calculators with keys to evaluate the trigonometric functions like the Texas Instruments TI-30 are used at the secondary level. A series of cards such as those in figure III.3 will reinforce the use of mental math.

Figure III.3

cos 73.5	**sin 19**	**tan 45**

1. 89 x 27	2. 25 x 17 x 4
3. 25% of 60	4. 2,979 + 6,215 + 87,567
5. 41,003 – 8,176	6. 12 x 5
7. 12 x 50	8. 9,287 ÷ 37
9. 98 x 47 + 2 x 47	10. 3/4 of 24

Figure III.4

After using their calculators for the first two computations, students will continue, in lemming-like fashion, to use their calculators to do the third one. When they obtain a display of 1, they will remember your constant admonition to "look before you leap." Try it again in the following weeks and many more students will use mental math.

Use flash cards to remind students that, in many cases, the human mind is quicker than a machine. Flash cards can be used as an effective warm-up at the beginning of a lesson, imbedded within a lesson, on those test days when a few minutes are left in the period, and on days when a special assembly program may shorten the math period.

QUICK STUFF

Prologue

As with the use of flash cards, activities like QUICK STUFF send the same message to students—"It's easier and faster to do this computation mentally." Use this type of activity several times during a semester. An important part of the lesson involves the dialogue that takes place after all students complete the activity and discuss the methods used to do each computation. Yes, you will have to prepare a handout but you want students to have a record of their work to keep in their notebooks for referral later in the year.

Procedure

Prepare a sheet of problems similar to the ten problems shown in figure III.4. The computations can be specific to the skills currently being taught or of a more general nature covering previously learned skills. The ones in figure III.4 are appropriate for middle school students in grades 6-8. Include about 30-40 computations. You may want to distribute the sheet of computations face down. Give the following directions: "Find the answers as quickly as you can. Ready? Go." Until students learn to "look before you leap," they will ask at this point, "Do we have to use our calculators?" Just repeat the above directions.

Keep track of the elapsed time for the first student to complete the problems. When all or most of the class have completed the problems, discuss with the class the answers and methods used. For the above sample of ten computations, it seems realistic that only three or four of them are calculator appropriate. Of course, this is a relative statement—for some of your students who have not been doing their jobs, all of the computations may be calculator appropriate!

Most of us would use a calculator to do the first one, answer: 2,403. Example 2: Rearrange using the associative and commutative properties of multiplication, 25 x 17 x 4 = 25 x 4 x 17 = 100 x 17 = 1,700. Example 3: 25% = 1/4; one-fourth of 60 is 15. Example 4: For many of us, this is not worth messing with—use a calculator, answer: 94,079. Example 5: Similar to the last one—I'd use a calculator, answer: 32,827. Example 6: Basic fact, answer: 60. Example 7: This is ten times the last answer, 600. Example 8: Need I say which is most appropriate to use? Answer: 251. Example 9: Tricky one—using the distributive property of multiplication over addition, this is the same as 100 x 47, answer: 4,700. Example 10: The denominator of the fraction divides the whole number—use mental math, answer: 18.

Have students discuss their methods. Determine if there is a relationship between elapsed time and total number of problems correct. Find the average time elapsed to complete the problems and average correct. Put results on a bulletin board and when you do additional Quick Stuff activities during the year, add to the chart.

Follow-Up

As you use Quick Stuff during the school year, students will use mental math more frequently as they get into the state of mind of "looking before they leap." By following up with consumer problems that lend themselves to the use of mental math, your students will continue to use calculators appropriately.

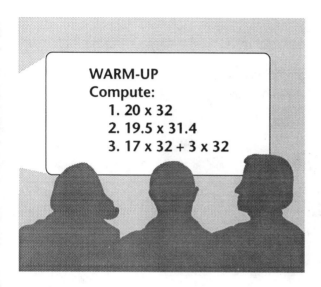

Figure III.5

WARM-UPS

Whether you call them warm-ups , pre-classwork, "to-dos" or whatever, the first five to eight minutes of a class period is perhaps the most important part of a lesson. This is the time to "get the juices flowing," to get students excited about mathematics. I kept a file folder of several hundred warm-ups cross-referenced with skills and concepts to be taught. Students knew that when they entered my room, there would be a warm-up on the overhead, blackboard, or easel for them to do. Other times, the warm-up would be directed by me. Either way, using a warm-up is an effective way to begin each and every class period.

One method of providing calculator-appropriate instruction during a transition period to a calculator-integrated curriculum is through warm-ups . Some teachers are comfortable with calculators on student desks at all times while others are still hesitant about "going all the way." The warm-up is a good place to start.

Emphasizing the use of mental-math strategies works well as warm-up activities. The use of flash cards as described earlier in this chapter is an example of a good starting activity at the beginning of class. Short versions of Quick Stuff can be used as warm-ups. Figure III.5 is an example of a warm-up focusing on appropriate computational methods.

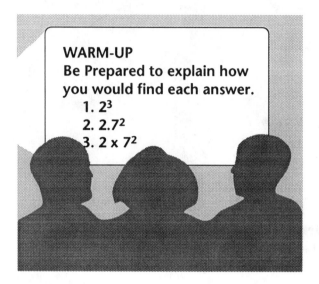

WARM-UP
Be Prepared to explain how
you would find each answer.
1. 2^3
2. 2.7^2
3. 2×7^2

Figure III.6

Students at the middle school level should be able to do the first one mentally arriving at a product of 640. The second one is calculator appropriate-but, students should reason that the product should be about 640. The correct product is 612.3. The third one is the same as $(17 + 3) \times 32 = 20 \times 32 = 640$.

Here is another warm-up involving exponents where the focus is on communicating methods of computing. (See Figure III.6.) If students are using journals, have them write several sentences for each example.

Warm-ups are short and sweet—and effective. Use them on a daily basis including ones that focus on appropriate use of calculators.

COMPETITIONS

Another way of "sneaking in" some mental math work is to conduct competitions between individuals or groups of students. Use the overhead projector so students see only one problem at a time. In a competition, quick and accurate answers are necessary. You can add a "game show" flavor by using bells, like the ones on counters of hotels, and requiring students to ring the bell when they have an answer. Include an awards ceremony, too. Award bonus points or extra credit points for individual or team winners.

1. 46 x 37 + 78	2. 78 + 46 x 37
3. 68% of 50	4. 0.375 x 40
5. 3,611 ÷ 157	6. 600 ÷ 15
7. 1,877 + 3,299 + 971	8. 330,037 − 291,778
9. 8^4	10. 89 x 45 + 11 x 45

Figure III.7

Combine knowledge of the calculator being used with mental-math strategies. For example, on a basic four-function calculator, the expression "87 + 23 x 56" cannot be keyed in directly for the correct answer of 1375. You want students to "look before they leap" and mentally transform the expression to "23 x 56 +87."

As correct answers are given, ask the student to explain how they processed the problem. This discussion is a valuable part of the competition. Figure III.7 shows a sample of ten problems from a competition for middle school students.

How many of the above can you do without a calculator? **1.** 1,780 **2.** Same as number 1, 1,780. **3.** Same as 50% of 68, 34. (See A Percent Puzzler in Chapter II.) **4.** Think "three-eighths of 40, 15. **5.** 23 **6.** 40 **7.** 6,147 **8.** 38,259 **9.** Most basic calculators have a constant function for multiplication.

Press 8 ⊠ ⊟ ⊟ ⊟ for a display of 4096. **10.** Same as 100 x 45, 4,500.

Try competitions with your students using appropriate computation and calculator skills.

ONE TO FIVE

Prologue

There are many variations of this activity that I use from time to time but I like this version the best. You can format the examples as equations to be completed or as sequences to be completed. It is formatted here as equations to be completed because the activity then is not dependent on a specific calculator. I use it as a "calculator" activi-

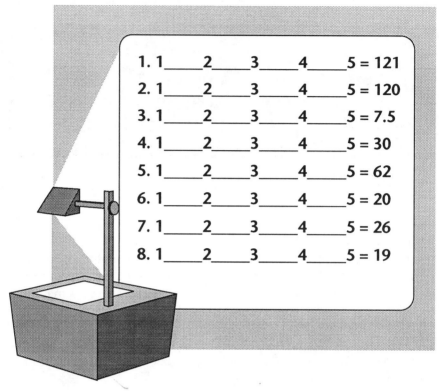

1. 1_____2_____3_____4_____5 = 121

2. 1_____2_____3_____4_____5 = 120

3. 1_____2_____3_____4_____5 = 7.5

4. 1_____2_____3_____4_____5 = 30

5. 1_____2_____3_____4_____5 = 62

6. 1_____2_____3_____4_____5 = 20

7. 1_____2_____3_____4_____5 = 26

8. 1_____2_____3_____4_____5 = 19

Figure III.8

ty even though I want students to use mental math as much as possible. Use this activity when working with order of operations.

Procedure

This activity will consist of two parts. For the first part, have the eight equations in figure III.8 on the chalkboard, overhead projector, or, if you must, prepare a handout for students.

Students must insert operations (+, −, x, ÷) to make each equation true. Yes, the same operation can be used more than once for each of the equations. Otherwise, some of the numbers would be unreachable—number sense at work! Make sure students understand the directions. Review order of operations. Then let students loose. As a solution

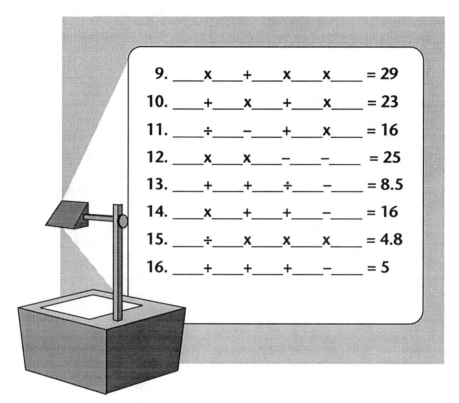

9. ____x____+____x____x____ = 29

10. ____+____x____+____x____ = 23

11. ____÷____–____+____x____ = 16

12. ____x____x____–____–____ = 25

13. ____+____+____÷____–____ = 8.5

14. ____x____+____+____–____ = 16

15. ____÷____x____x____x____ = 4.8

16. ____+____+____+____–____ = 5

Figure III.9

is found, have the student come to the chalkboard and fill in the missing operations.

Answers: There are alternate answers to some of the equations. Here is a set of possible answers. **1.** In order, +, x, x, x **2.** x, x, x, x **3.** x, x, ÷, x **4.** ÷, x, x, x **5.** x, +, x, x **6.** +, x, x, – **7.** x, x, +, x **8.** x, +, x, +

After you review the results of the above, turn the tables with the eight equations in figure III.9.

Students must use the digits (1, 2, 3, 4, 5) in any order to make true equations. Again, order of operations must be considered. Each of the above adheres to the order of operations; no parentheses are needed. Have students fill in the missing numbers as each equation is completed.

Answers: There may be other possibilities. **9.** In order, 5, 1, 2, 3, 4

10. 1, 3, 4, 2, 5 **11.** 4, 2, 1, 3, 5 **12.** 2, 3, 5, 4, 1 **13.** 3, 4, 5, 2, 1 **14.** 3, 4, 5, 1, 2 **15.** 1, 5, 2, 3, 4 **16.** 1, 2, 3, 4, 5

Follow-Up

Some students will "peck away" with their calculators if they have not yet learned to "look before they leap." Others will use mental math without use of their calculators. In fact, some students using mental math will not do the equations in order. They will scan the entire set using mental math and number sense mentally rearranging the operations or numbers to arrive at the correct choices. Discuss strategies at the end of each part of the activity.

Use shortened versions of this activity as warm-ups throughout the year. Use less numbers and operations. With four numbers and three operations, you can use the digits in the current year or a famous year like 1492. Use of parentheses adds to the possibilities.

SUMMARY

Whether you have primary students with basic calculators or precalculus students armed with graphing calculators in front of you eagerly awaiting your words of wisdom, you need to teach mental-math strategies and use these strategies during your instruction. In a technological classroom, mental math is as important as ever. If an exact answer is necessary, students need to choose an appropriate method of computation. Make sure mental math is one of those choices. You can help them develop a state of mind, a brief pause to consider if a computation can be processed using mental arithmetic. Remember to teach "look before you leap."

CHAPTER IV

Estimation

INTRODUCTION

We estimate either when an exact answer is not necessary or when we want to know if a subsequent calculation, whether to be performed using paper and pencil or using a calculator, will be "in the ballpark." The trouble is that students and many adults simply do not estimate before doing involved computations. And, of course, they have no idea if their answer is reasonable.

It was bad enough in a non-calculator classroom, but with calculators being used, it is crucial that students learn how to estimate. Students have a false sense of security when using calculators. "The display must be correct." Good teaching can change this attitude.

You want students to estimate before performing a calculation. It's difficult to assess whether students are estimating answers. I remember giving quizzes and providing spaces for estimates and exact answers. Students were instructed to estimate and then find exact answers. In observing students during these quizzes, I would watch them do a computation, write it down in the space for the exact answer and then "fudge it" up or down and fill in the space for the estimate after they have already figured out the exact answer. That process is of little value.

If students have learned rounding skills and have developed a sense of number, then they can be taught to estimate and use estimates to determine whether answers are reasonable. Force them to estimate. One way of forcing students to estimate is to play "Estimation Derby."

ESTIMATION DERBY

Prologue

This activity can be used at any level using appropriate computational skills. Once you use the activity students will want to play it

	Round 1	Round 2	Round 3	Round 4	Round 5	
Estimate						
Exact Answer						Total Score
Difference						

Figure IV.1

often. If you play Estimation Derby once a week for several weeks and then on a less-often basis, students' estimation skills improve dramatically. Use it as a whole class activity.

Procedure

Provide each student with a score sheet (see figure IV.1). You can put as many as six of these on a 8.5 x 11 sheet of paper and use a paper cutter to cut the individual score sheets. Save the master; you will use it many times during the year. The score sheet includes space for five rounds of estimations, but you can use as few as three rounds as an effective warm-up at the beginning of a lesson or a new unit.

Explain to students that you are going to show them computations; their task is to estimate the answer and write it in the space for round 1's estimate. Then you will show the computation again and students will find the exact answer. Their score for round 1 will be the difference between the estimate and the exact answer. More precisely, the score will be the absolute value of the difference between the estimate and the exact answer. You want a positive number for the score–"big number on top..." You will do this for five rounds. At the end of the five rounds, students total their differences. Low score wins.

Now each of your students may be thinking, "This is going to be a snap. I'll find the exact answer and each of my scores will be zero."

You have a trick in store for them. Have your computations prepared on projectuals for the overhead projector. You show the first one (see figure IV.2) but only for a few seconds and cover it up quickly.

They must estimate; there will not be time to find the exact answer. Now there will be groans from your students; tease them with another fast look. All students must write down an estimate. They are in competition with each other so each will make sure everyone declares in

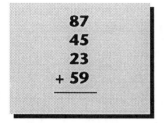

Figure IV.2

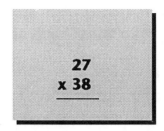

Figure IV.3

writing an estimate. After estimates are declared, survey the class for their estimates. Remind students that with estimates, they won't get wrong answers; some are just better than others. Then show the computation and have students determine the exact answer and their scores for round 1. Discuss techniques at this point. Depending on the time you gave them to estimate, you want students to be able to "see" 100 (group 87 and 23) and 100 (group 45 and 59) for an estimate of 200. They may not have enough time to round each addend to the nearest ten. Make sure students understand how to determine their score for the first round. Proceed to round 2. A possible computation for the second round is given in figure IV.3.

The multiplication in figure IV.3 gives you the opportunity to develop good number sense. As they have been taught, students will round both factors to the nearest ten, 30 and 40, for an estimate of 1,200. Ask them if both factors are rounded up as in this case, won't the estimated product be greater than the exact product? A more precise estimate will result if one factor is rounded up and one down—as in 25 x 40, which can be computed mentally, 1,000. The exact answer is 1,026.

After five rounds, students' final scores will be the sum of their five differences. Low score wins—isn't it refreshing when the lowest total is the winner?

Follow-Up

Students can have the most sophisticated calculator that is available on their desks and it won't help in playing Estimation Derby. Students are "forced" to use estimation. Their scores will improve with each time the game is played. Estimation Derby can be played at all levels from elementary school mathematics to secondary topics. And when students are using their calculators to do an application involving a complex calculation, they just may estimate before they use their calculators; and that's the point of playing Estimation Derby!

BE REASONABLE

Prologue

Once you have sensitized students to the need to estimate, you can do a variety of estimation activities during the school year. Start your lesson with an estimation warm-up. Use the computational skills being studied as the basis of your estimation warm-up or provide a cumulative-type warm-up using computational skills learned to date. The warm-up described here is appropriate for students who have studied order of operations.

Incidentally, even in advanced mathematics classes, students need to use mental math, computational and estimation skills frequently while working on their "regular" stuff. Recently I was at an archery shoot and halfway through the course, stopped in the clubhouse for a hot dog and soda. I treated my friend and ordered two hot dogs and two sodas. The hot dogs were $1.50 each and sodas were 50 cents each. I gave the young man behind the counter a five-dollar bill and he gave me two dollar bills in change. I told the young man that he gave me too much change, that the total was four dollars ($3 + $1). He thanked me but then rationalized his error by saying, "I don't do this kind of math, I'm taking pre-calculus." My friend was amused but I did a slow burn.

Procedure

I like to have my warm-ups already on the chalkboard so that when the students enter the room, they know exactly what to do. In this case, I make an exception and may have on the board, "Get ready, a Be Reasonable is on the way." Once I enter the room I put the prepared warm-up (see figure IV.4) on the overhead. In this manner, I can control the time and be confident that the students estimate rather than find exact answers.

For the first one, some students are quick enough to use mental math and determine the exact answer—6 x 50 + 87 - 6 = 381. For the rest of us mortals, I am satisfied if students "see" 300 + 100 = 400 as a reasonable estimate. Furthermore, I want them to use number sense and know that an estimate of 400 will be greater than the exact answer.

> A. Estimate each of the following:
>
> 1. 6 x 49 + 87 =
>
> 2. 17 x 29 + 42 x 19 =
>
> 3. 27 x 32 − 24 x 5 =
>
> B. Find the exact answers for each of the above. Compare your answers in A and B. Are your estimates reasonable? Compare your estimates with a classmate's estimates.

Figure IV.4

For the second example, I want students to "see" 600 (20 x 30) + 800 (40 x 20) = 1,400 as a reasonable estimate. Similarly, for the third one, students should think 900 (30 x 30) - 100 (20 x 5) = 800.

Follow-Up

The discussion among students comparing their estimates is desirable for encouraging communication in mathematics. Use this type of warm-up frequently through the year. Here's another quickie to use to encourage estimation.

ORDER, PLEASE

Prologue

At times, an exact answer is not necessary, an estimate is sufficient to get the job done. Estimation skills and number sense are reinforced with warm-ups such as this one.

Procedure

Have figure IV.5 on the chalkboard or overhead. Control time if students still are not estimating. If you do not want to limit time, some students will find exact answers—others will use estimation skills and

Arrange in order, from largest to smallest:

1. 23.4 + 0.85

2. 23.4 x 0.85

3. 23.4 ÷ 0.85

Figure IV.5

number sense. Having done it both ways, I think either method is effective. Both the "exact answer" group and the "estimators" will get the correct order. The difference is that the "estimators" will do a lot less work with pencil and paper or with their calculators. Remember from the section on mental math, "Look before you leap." 23.4 x 0.85 will be the smallest of the three because a number (23.4) is being multiplied by a number less than one, so the product will be less than 23.4. The sum of 23.4 and 0.85 will be a little larger than 23.4 and 23.4 divided by a number less than 1 will be larger than the other two calculations. By using estimation, number sense, and reasoning, no actual computation is involved. From largest to smallest: 23.4 ÷ 0.85, 23.4 + 0.85, 23.4 x 0.85.

Follow-Up

Provide similar warm-ups throughout the year. Have students explain their reasoning in ordering the expressions. This type of activity helps students develop good number sense and estimation skills.

DOT'S RIGHT

Prologue

This warm-up can also be expanded and used as a full-fledged activity. Use it when working with operations with decimals. Once students are in the "thinking mode" and using estimation skills, no calculations are necessary except to verify choices.

> The right side of the equation is correct. The left side needs a decimal point. Place the decimal point in the correct position.
>
> 1. 275 x 52.4 = 144.1
>
> 2. 560.868 ÷ 924 = 6.07
>
> 3. (17.5 + 23.4) x 145 = 59.305

Figure IV.6

Procedure

Use figure IV.6 as a warm-up. Make sure students understand that you did not make any mistakes; the left side of each equation needs a decimal point. Students need to place the decimal point on the left sides of each equation to make them true.

Since one of the numbers (52.4) on the left side of the first equation already has a decimal point, work with the other number. Think: 3 x 50 = 150, so the decimal point must be placed between the "2" and the "7" producing the number, 2.75. For the second example, think: 560 ÷ 100 = 5.6, so the number must be 92.4. Verify using a calculator. You have really built students' comfort levels when they tell you they don't have to verify their choices! For the last one, think: 40 x 1 = 40 and 40 x 10 = 400, so the number must be 1.45.

Follow-Up

Try this extension. If you use two numbers on the left side and show no decimal points, you create a more open-ended activity where there is more than one answer. For example, try 34 x 23 = 78.2. Possible answers include 3.4 x 23 and 34 x 2.3.

Dot's Right can help students better understand operations with decimals and improve their estimation skills.

SUMMARY

Quite simply, good estimation skills are crucial if students are going to use calculators efficiently and accurately regardless of whether they are using a basic calculator like the TI-108 or a graphing calculator like the TI-81.

Rounding skills are taught throughout the grades as students learn computational skills. These rounding skills are used to estimate answers to computations. Students must be able to determine whether answers to calculator calculations are reasonable and "in the ballpark." Teach your students to estimate before they start to "peck away" at the keys of their calculators.

In a problem situation, if a calculation and exact answer are needed, and if the use of a calculator is the most appropriate method of computation, then teach your students to estimate before they use their calculators and to compare estimates and answers after use of calculators.

Use of technology and the importance of estimation are recognized in the recommendations of the NCTM Standards. You can help students to use calculators efficiently if you stress estimation skills in your lessons.

CHAPTER V

Number Crunching

INTRODUCTION

The term "number crunching" has been attached to any onerous task involving the manipulation of many and often, large numbers. Accountants "crunch out numbers" in determining the "bottom line." Researchers "crunch numbers" using computers to run exhaustive searches of number patterns.

I use the term "number crunching" to describe classroom activities involving large numbers. These activities are well suited for using calculators. Calculators handle the drudgery of working with "messy" computations with large numbers, enabling students to concentrate on exploring patterns with numbers and problem solving.

Students like working with large numbers. Without calculators, many do not have the skill proficiency and perseverance to compute with large numbers and are deprived of many rich explorations. Use a variety of activities and investigations such as those given in this section to provide opportunities for students to explore operations with large numbers. You will be pleasantly surprised at the speed with which many students find solutions to problems and activities involving large numbers. They will be involved in exhaustive searches, organizing data, working with patterns, and engaged in the process of problem solving.

PRODUCT EXPLORATION

Prologue

This investigation can be used any time after students have worked with multiplication of whole numbers. It involves a search for largest products of multi-digit factors. There is reasoning and number sense involved with this activity; students also learn to keep an organized list

There are ten digits below. Use these digits to fill
the blanks in each multiplication. Tour aim: try to
make the *largest* possible products. Here's the
catch: you may use a digit once in each problem.
Good exploring!

0, 1, 2, 3, 4, 5, 6, 7, 8, 9

Product

1. ___ ___ ___ x ___   1. _____

2. ___ ___ x ___ ___   2. _____

3. ___ ___ ___ x ___ ___   3. _____

4. ___ ___ ___ x ___ ___ ___ 4. _____

5. ___ ___ ___ ___ x ___ ___ ___ 5. _____

6. ___ ___ ___ ___ x ___ ___ ___ ___ 6. _____

Figure V.1

of their work, a necessity even in a technological world. You can
extend this activity using other operations. Use as a cooperative learning experience and have each team report on its findings.

Procedure

Provide each team with a handout or have figures V.1 and V.2 prepared on the overhead or chalkboard.

Spend a few minutes familiarizing teams with the directions. Make
sure they understand that 999 x 9 is not an acceptable answer for the
first problem; they must use four different digits. If you give the teams
both sets of problems at the same time, remind them that for the sec-

Use the same digits. This time, find the *smallest* products possible.

	Product
7. ___ ___ ___ ___ x ___	7. _____
8. ___ ___ x ___ ___	8. _____
9. ___ ___ ___ x ___ ___	9. _____
10. ___ ___ ___ x ___ ___ ___	10. _____
11. ___ ___ ___ ___ x ___ ___	11. _____
12. ___ ___ ___ ___ x ___ ___ ___ ___	12. _____

Figure V.2

ond set, the object is to minimize the products. Now turn them loose!

After groups have completed the investigation, provide time for each team to report out their findings.

Answers: **1.** 876 x 9 = 7,884; **2.** 96 x 87 = 8,352;
3. 875 x 96 = 84,000; **4.** 964 x 875 = 843,500;
5. 8,754 x 96 = 840,384; **6.** 9,642 x 8,753 = 84,396,426
7. The one-digit number is 0; **8.** 23 x 10 = 230;
9. 234 x 10 = 2,340; **10.** 235 x 104 = 24,440;
11. 2,345 x 10 = 23,450; **12.** 2,457 x 1036 = 2,545,452

Follow-Up

As you observe the groups at work, especially if students have not been involved in similar experiences, they may demonstrate a lack of reasoning ability and number sense. Many will "peck away" at keys not keeping track of the different combinations they have tried. Many will be convinced that for the first problem, using the four largest digits in descending order to form two factors will result in the largest product (987 x 6).

Other teams will reason that you need to use the four largest digits but will "play" with them trying different combinations till they find the one that results in the largest product (876 x 9 = 7,884). With the second problem, they may start to see a pattern. They also keep track of their trials.

This type of search illustrates the obvious advantage of using calculators. Though not impossible to complete using paper and pencil, it would be an extremely tedious task. With calculators, students can concentrate on pattern exploration and not get bogged down, and frustrated, with the computations involved. Students have fun working on this investigation which encompasses many of the recommendations contained in the NCTM Standards.

RING TOSS

Prologue

If you are in tight with the shop teacher, have him/her make you a ring-toss board as shown in figure V.3. A wood base and dowels are all you need.

You can use number tags to label each dowel; change the numbers and use again during the year. Use rubber gaskets from pickle bottles

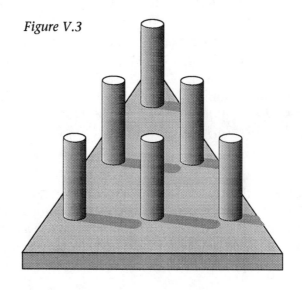

Figure V.3

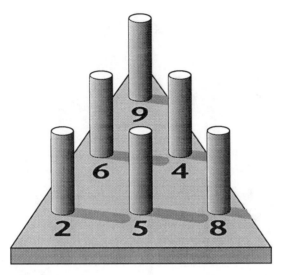

Figure V.4

for "rings." Have students toss the gaskets at the board and see if they can ring the dowels.

Procedure

If you and the shop teacher are not on good terms, draw a large copy of the ring-toss board on posterboard. If you laminate it, you can use a grease pencil on top of the lamination to number the dowels. In this manner, you can change the numbers to create additional activities or work with different ability groups. The ring-toss board can be used at varied levels—use smaller numbers with elementary students.

I taught in an older building which had large windows. Large windows have large window shades. I taped the laminated ring-toss board (using construction paper so it would bend) to the window shades and rolled up the shade. I would walk over to the window side of the room and dramatically pull the shade down to start my lesson. I had other puzzles on the other window shades so students were never quite sure which shade I was going to pull down. Check with your principal if you want to utilize the window shades for additional space for activities and displays!

Start off this "number cruncher" with a mental-math activity (see figure V.4). Your students have to assume "rings" are tossed at the

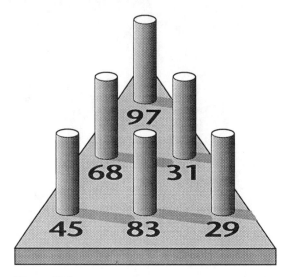

Figure V.5

board and that there are no "misses." A score represents the sum of the numbered dowels that are ringed.

Ask the following:

1. "Throw three rings for a score of 11." (2, 5, 4) Some students will give you the pair 9, 2 or the pair 5, 6 but you said "three" rings.
2. "Throw three rings for a score of 23." (9, 6, 8 or 9, 9, 5)
3. "Throw four rings for a score of 24." (2, 5, 8, 9 or 4, 5, 6, 9 or 6, 6, 6, 6)
4. "Throw five rings for a score of 36." (2, 8, 8, 9, 9 or 4, 8, 8, 8, 8 or 2, 4, 9, 9, 9)

Now you are ready for some "number crunching." Use figure V.5–pull down the next window shade!

Use cooperative-learning groups for the balance of the lesson. Have the following questions on the chalkboard or overhead:

1. Use three rings for a score of 173.
2. Use four rings for a score of 277.
3. Use four rings for a score of 210.
4. Use five rings for a score of 335.

Provide time for groups to report on their findings. Possible answers include:

1. 45, 31, 97;
2. 29, 68, 83, 97;
3. 29, 45, 68, 68;
4. 29, 29, 83, 97, 97.

Follow-Up

I am continually amazed at the speed with which some teams of students arrive at all answers and eagerly ask for more problems. Have the teams make up additional ring-toss scores for the other teams to do.

With two-digit dowels, students use estimation skills to help them get "in the ballpark" then "crunch" numbers with their calculators to find the correct scores. Another strategy students use is to find the sum of all numbered dowels and work backwards. This method is most successful when there are no "doubles" or "triples."

When you use activities like Ring Toss, you create a classroom atmosphere that fosters student interaction. Your students will want to come to math class and see what surprises await them. Keep changing those window shades!

ADDITION AND MULTIPLICATION TRAILS

Prologue

Now let's do some serious "number crunching." Every time students successfully complete one of these, I ask them how they did it, what strategy did they use. Invariably, the answer will be, "I don't know, I just guessed." Though it is difficult to assess number sense, I am sure that these students have a firm grasp of number sense and good estimation skills to be successful with these activities.

Addition and multiplication-trail activities can be used anytime after students learn to compute with these two operations. The complexity of the mazes and size of the numbers in the mazes are determined by the skill level of students. With algebra students, I prepared similar trail activities using variables for students to manipulate.

Procedure

These activities work well in an activity corner. Copy the number puzzles on oaktag and laminate. By making sets of these puzzles, you can use a specific puzzle determined by an individual student's or team's skill level. Of course you can copy the puzzles on a master and

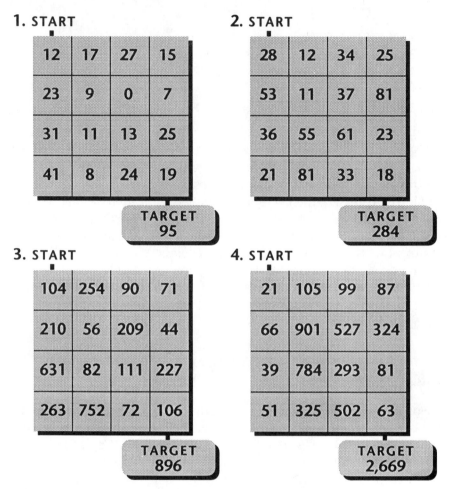

1. START

12	17	27	15
23	9	0	7
31	11	13	25
41	8	24	19

TARGET
95

2. START

28	12	34	25
53	11	37	81
36	55	61	23
21	81	33	18

TARGET
284

3. START

104	254	90	71
210	56	209	44
631	82	111	227
263	752	72	106

TARGET
896

4. START

21	105	99	87
66	901	527	324
39	784	293	81
51	325	502	63

TARGET
2,669

Figure V.6

make copies for your class. Designate a day as "trail day" and provide many addition and multiplication trails of varying complexity. Let's deal with addition first.

Here are four addition puzzles for students to "trail" through. (See Figure V.6.)

Prepare an oaktag direction board. (See figure V.7.)

Students must follow the rules and make a trail to the target numbers. Students start with the number in the "START" box. Legal moves involve down, over, and up moves. No diagonal moves are permitted. The instruction, "You cannot cross your trail." implies that the same

> ## RULES
>
> * Add the numbers on your trail.
> * You cannot cross your trail.
> * You must travel up, down, or to the side.
> * You cannot travel on the diagonal.

Figure V.7

number cannot be used more than one time. As students make a trail, they add the numbers in the boxes. The object is to reach the target sum.

Many students will use mental math to work through the first puzzle. As the puzzles increase in difficulty, the advantage of having a calculator becomes apparent. One strategy students quickly pick up is that the number in the box directly above the target number will be included in the trail. Others will find the sum of all sixteen numbers in the puzzle and then selectively subtract numbers till they near the target number. In cooperative groups students will portion out different trails to members of the group to test.

Have students discuss their work after all trails are determined. This dialogue is an important part of this activity. Possible answers include:

    1. 12-17-9-0-13-25-19
    2. 28-53-36-55-61-33-18
    3. 104-254-90-71-44-227-106
    4. 21-105-901-784-293-502-63

Now, have students do some "trail work" with multiplication puzzles. (See Figure V.8.)

Make sure students understand the directions; this time, they multiply numbers. For each puzzle, students start with the number in the "START" box. Legal moves involve down, over, and up moves. No diagonal moves are permitted. The instruction, "You cannot cross your trail" implies that the same number cannot be used more than one time. As students make a trail, they multiply the numbers in the boxes. The object is to reach the target product.

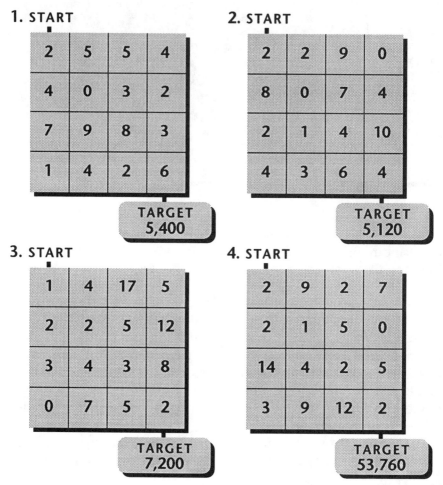

Figure V.8

Many students will "peck away" hoping to hit the target. Others will use estimation skills. Knowledge of factors and multiples will be used. There are boxes with "0" in them which should assist students in limiting trail choices. Students will also use the "1" factors to limit the size of the product. A successful strategy is to factor the target product and try to find a trail with the correct factors—but don't tell your students; let them explore.

One strategy students quickly pick up is that the number in the box directly above the target number will be included in the trail. Students will learn to not use the larger numbers as factors as the final products will be too large. Remind students how to clear an error. In cooperative groups students will portion out different trails to members of the group to test.

As with the addition trails, have students discuss their work after all trails are determined. This dialogue is an important part of this activity. Possible answers include:

1. 2-5-5-3-2-3-6
2. 2-8-2-1-4-10-4
3. 1-2-3-4-2-5-3-5-2
4. 2-2-14-4-1-5-2-12-2

Follow-Up

You can use the addition puzzles as one multi-day project and the multiplication puzzles as another multi-day project. Remember the window shades? You can put oaktag copies on the window shades and use individual puzzles as warm-ups or "rainy-day" activities. Students use mental math, estimation, and number-sense skills to help them start to solve these puzzles. When "the going gets rough," the calculator is used to finish them off.

MILLION MADNESS

Prologue

In today's economy, a million, as in one million dollars, is not as big a number as it was years ago. In fact, years ago, when I first started to use one of the problems in this activity, I referred to a few pro basketball players earning $1,000,000. Today, the average pro basketball player makes $1,000,000. Times have changed—a theme of this book.

With access to calculators, students have the opportunity to explore problems involving large numbers. Large numbers are all around them—salaries of rock stars and entertainers, federal deficits, etc. Take advantage of these large numbers and provide "number-crunching" activities.

Announce ahead of time, a day devoted to problems involving a million—or if inflation continues to grow, call it a two-million day. Build anticipation with classroom signs announcing that "million day is coming."

Procedure

Use cooperative groups for this activity. With the availability of calculators, students will be able to concentrate on problem-solving skills and not have to deal with tedious computations. Use newspapers and almanacs to find interesting facts involving the number one million.

Before the groups start work, have each group declare an estimate—the range of estimations will amaze you. After the activity is completed and you review work with your students, return to the estimates and see who was closest to the exact answers. Here are some sample "million" problems.

1. If it were possible, how many days would it take to count to 1,000,000 at the rate of a number a second?
2. The average basketball player earns a salary of $1,000,000. A game lasts 48 minutes. If a $1,000,000 player plays every minute of every game in a 72-game season, what is his pay per minute?
3. How many days would it take to spend $1,000,000 if you spent $5 per second, 8 hours a day?
4. A normal heart beats 72 times a minute. How many days will it take to beat 1,000,000 times?
5. If possible, what would be the combined length in miles of 1,000,000 dollar bills layed end to end?

Five to eight problems similar to the above will provide students with ample material for discussion in a cooperative-learning setup. After all groups have completed their work, provide time for discussion of their answers. These problems provide students with an opportunity to use rates, recall implicit information, choose the correct operation(s), use higher-order thinking skills and work effectively as a group.

For problem 1, 1,000,000 ÷ 60 yields the rate per minute. Dividing that result by 60 gives the rate per hour, and finally, dividing this quotient by 24 yields the rate per day or the number of days it would take to count to 1,000,000 at the rate of a number a second—with no rests! 1,000,000 ÷ 60 ÷ 60 ÷ 24 = 11.574073. So, it would take about 11.5 days. Review the estimates. Is anyone close? Review other methods that students may have used.

For problem 2, students may use different methods but there are a total of 3,456 minutes in 72 games—assuming no overtimes! 1,000,000 ÷ 3,456 = 289.35185. So, an average player makes about $290 a minute. Since most of these average players play less than 48 minutes in each game, their pay per minutes played is usually much more than $290. This provides a good extension of this problem. Check the box scores of pro basketball games to see the number of minutes played by players. Revise the numbers for a team's roster.

For problem 3, in an 8-hour day, one could spend $144,000 at the rate of $5 per second (8 x 60 x 60 x 5). Dividing $1,000,000 by this rate yields 6.9444444. So, it would take about 7 days. Happy shopping!

For problem 4, dividing 1,000,000 by the rate per minute gives the total number of minutes (13,888.888). Dividing this by 60 gives the number of hours, and finally, dividing that answer by 24 gives the number of days, 9.6450608. It would take about 9.6 days.

A dollar bill measures about 6.1875 inches. Let's round this off to 6.2 inches. Layed end-to-end, these bills would cover 6,200,000 inches. Divide by 12 to get the number of feet (516,666.66). Finally, dividing by 5,280 gives us the number of miles (97.853534). So, a million one-dollar bills layed end-to-end would cover about 98 miles! Students have a difficult time believing this one. Try convincing them by covering the floor with ten bills, measure the length and then multiply this length by 100,000 and the result will be the same.

Follow-Up

Begin a file of interesting problems involving a million and other large numbers. Use problems from the file as warm-ups or for another "million day." Students will suggest rich extensions to explore. Once again, "number crunching" activities can be informative and fun, and more importantly, accessible to all of your students with the aid of calculators.

SUMMARY

Traditional curriculum practices have shied away from computations involving large numbers. The availability and use of calculators has changed this practice. Using a scientific calculator such as the Texas Instruments TI-30 Challenger, which converts numbers that exceed the display's 8-digit capacity to scientific notation, allows students to work effectively with very large and very small numbers.

Include "number-crunching" activities in your "bag of tricks." The use of calculators empowers students to explore the realm of large numbers and concentrate on mathematics, and not on tedious computations.

CHAPTER VI

Patterns

INTRODUCTION

If you have been working through this book chapter by chapter, then you have seen the focus on recognizing number patterns in mathematics. Studying patterns in mathematics helps one better understand the structure of number systems. Many mathematicians define mathematics as the study of patterns. Exploring number patterns is a significant part of pre-college mathematics and cited in the NCTM Standards as a major focus of school mathematics.

As with "number-crunching" activities, using calculators when exploring number patterns empowers students to concentrate on reasoning skills and not spend inordinate time with computations. Students are more apt to try hunches with calculators, to determine where a path might lead. The pattern investigations in this chapter assume calculators are available to students and will be used when needed.

This chapter could easily be the largest chapter in this book but we have already worked with patterns and will do so again in this book. Only two investigations are in this chapter because they are my favorite pattern activities with calculators.

TWO DIGITS FROM THREE DIGITS

Prologue

This investigation can be used anytime after students have learned place value to four and five digits and addition skills with three and four digits. With algebra students, you can include an algebraic rationale for generalizations. If you are big on grade designations, I have used this investigation with third graders and with algebra students.

I like to prepare a master with five or six rows of the digits from 0 to

9. Then when I need digit cards for students to manipulate, I run off a few copies of the sheet and cut the sheets so each student has a strip with the digits from 0 to 9.

Procedure

The initial part of this investigation is teacher directed. Distribute digit strips to your students. Have them cut the strips so they have ten "cards" from 0 to 9. Regardless of the age of your students, this "manipulative" experience is enjoyed by all of them. Discard the "0" card. This is not necessary but makes the investigation easier to complete. Use these instructions.

1. "Use three of the cards to form a three-digit number." e.g., 372
2. "Find all the two-digit numbers you can from the three digits in this three-digit number. No repeat digits."
    37, 32, 72, 73, 23, 27
3. "Now find the sum of the two-digit numbers."
    37 + 32 + 72 + 73 + 23 + 27 = 264
4. "Now, find the sum of the three digits in your original three-digit number."
    3 + 7 + 2 = 12
5. "Divide the sum of the two-digit numbers by this sum."
    264 ÷ 12 = 22

Students will be amazed that regardless of each of their three-digit numbers, they all have 22. Have students try the procedure again with a different three-digit number. The results will all be the same, 22. They also learn quickly the need for paper and pencil in a technological classroom to keep an organized list of their numbers.

Now you are ready to "knock their socks off."

1. "This time, use four of the cards to form a four-digit number. e.g., 1,548
2. "Find all the two-digit numbers you can from the four digits in this four-digit number. No repeat digits."
    15, 14, 18, 54, 58, 51, 48, 41, 45, 81, 85, 84
3. "Now find the sum of the two-digit numbers."
    15 + 14 + 18 + 54 + 58 + 51 + 48 + 41 + 45 + 81 + 85 + 84 = 594
4. "Now, find the sum of the four digits in your original four-digit number."
    1 + 5 + 4 + 8 = 18

5. "Divide the sum of the two-digit numbers by this sum."
   $594 \div 18 = 33$

Students once again will be amazed that regardless of each of their four-digit numbers, they all have 33. Have students try the procedure again with a different four-digit number. The results will all be the same, 33.

"Now, let's see what happens for two-digit numbers."

1. "This time, use two of the cards to form a two-digit number."
   e.g., 93
2. "Find all the two-digit numbers you can from the two digits in this two-digit number. No repeat digits."
   93, 39
3. "Now find the sum of the two-digit numbers."
   $93 + 39 = 132$
4. "Now, find the sum of the two digits in your original two-digit number."
   $9 + 3 = 12$
5. "Divide the sum of the two-digit numbers by this sum."
   $132 \div 12 = 11$

Regardless of the two-digit numbers students chose, their results will be 11. Have students try the procedure again with a different two-digit number. The results will all be the same, 11.

Have students follow the procedure with a five-digit number. There will be 20 two-digit numbers possible. Students will tell you before they do the work that the final result will be 44. Make sure they find all possible two-digit numbers that can be formed from a five-digit number of five different non-zero digits.

To generalize, make a table of values for the four cases the students have explored.

"What would the result be if you started with a six-digit number?"
Students will respond, "55."

"What would the result be if you started with a seven-digit number?"
Students will respond, "66."

Here is a good opportunity to use the power of the computer and write a program for the above two procedures. This is an example of where the computer would be the most appropriate choice for computation.

For students who have had some experience with variables, ask "Suppose you had a n-digit number. How could we denote the result?"

No. of digits	Result
2	11
3	22
4	33
5	44
n	11(n-1)

Figure VI.1

Generalizing, some students will respond, "Multiply 11 by one less than the number of digits." Symbolically, 11 x (n - 1).

Follow-Up

For students with algebra skills, you can provide an algebraic rationale; keep it simple and show a rationale for one case. Use the first one from above.

1. Form a three-digit number abc; a, b, c $\in$ {1, 2, 3, ... 9}.
2. Form two-digit numbers from abc and expand the numbers.
   10a + b
   10a + c
   10b + c
   10b + a
   10c + a
   10c + b
3. Find the sum of the two-digit numbers and simplify.
   10a + b + 10a + c + 10b + c + 10b + a + 10c + a + 10c + b = 22a + 22b + 22c = 22 (a + b + c)
4. Find the sum of the three digits in the original three-digit number.
   a + b + c
5. Divide the sum of the two-digit numbers by this sum.
   22 (a + b + c) ÷ (a + b + c) = 22

Similar rationales can be provided for the other cases. Recapping, students began with a pattern search, generalized, and worked through an algebraic rationale with the teacher.

The explorations need not stop here. Once, with a sixth grade class, a student asked, "What would happen if we formed three-digit numbers from three, four, and five-digit numbers?" I was excited and said, "I don't know—let's see."

1. "Use three of the cards to form a three-digit number."
   e.g., 634
2. "Find all the three-digit numbers you can from the three digits in this three-digit number. No repeat digits."
   634, 643, 346, 364, 463, 436
3. "Now find the sum of the three-digit numbers."
   634 + 643 + 346 + 364 + 463 + 436 = 2,886
4. "Now, find the sum of the four digits in your original four-digit number."
   6 + 3 + 4 = 13
5. "Divide the sum of the two-digit numbers by this sum."
   2,886 ÷ 13 = 222

Students tried many different three-digit numbers but the result was the same each time-222. Many said, "It's 111 multiplied by 2, one less than the number of digits in the original number." Calculators in hand, they tackled a four-digit number with three-digit subsets. With 24 three-digit numbers this is quite a task. They used an organized list to keep track of all the numbers. And sure enough, they were delighted when they arrived at a final result of 666. While students saw that 666 is a multiple of 222 and 111, they were unable to figure out the generalization. Several intrepid students worked on five-digit numbers with three-digit subsets for a final result of 1332, which is 111 x 12. Though above the level of these sixth graders, the general pattern is 111 x (n - 1) (n - 2) for a n-digit number.

Nevertheless, they enjoyed following up on a classmate's "what if.." question and discovered a continuation of a pattern. What if you start with a four-digit number and form sets of four-digit numbers; what will the procedure yield? That's for the computer and another investigation!

NINES AND MORE NINES

Prologue

There are so many patterns involving 9's that I suggest you do what I have done several times—throw a "9 day" for your classes. Use a teacher-directed approach or set up "booths" around the room for students to rotate through as they explore patterns with 9's. Stock each "booth" with a pattern search on laminated oaktag.

This activity is appropriate for middle school students. The rationale for the first activity requires some understanding of repeating decimals. The beginning activity, unlike all other activities in this book, will only work on basic calculators which truncate displays. On calculators with displays that round off, such as the TI-12 Math Explorer, repeating decimals greater than 0.5 are rounded up—you will not get all "sixes" in the display for 2 ÷ 3.

Procedure

Whether or not you plan to set up "booths," direct this first activity. When the students enter the room and are ready for work, announce that you are going to play "No Eight." Ask a student for his/her favorite number from 1 to 9.

A student responds, "4."

You tell all to key in 1.2345679 ⨯ 36 ⊟

All displays read 44.444444.

On a calculator such as the MathMate with an automatic constant for multiplication, it is not necesary to enter 1.2345679 again. Students will ask why the activity is called "No Eight." "Look at the first factor you keyed in (1.2345679). Do you see an "8?"

"Give me another favorite number from 1 to 9."

"7"

"Everybody, key in 63 ⊟."

All displays will read 77.777777.

"Another favorite number."

Student: "2."

"Everybody, key in 18 ⊟."

All displays read 22.222222.

"Jimmy—what's your favorite number from 1 to 9?"

Jimmy responds with "5."

You instruct all to key in 45 ⊟.

All displays will read 55.555555.

By now, many of the class will be on to you. Determine whether they "see something" by asking, "My favorite number is 7. What do I key in?"

You will hear, "Press 63 =."

Displays will read 77.777777.

Now more will join in. "I want to see all 9's. Press 81 =."

Sure enough, students' displays will read 99.999999.

Another student says, "To see all 3's, press 27 =."

The displays will read 33.333333.

Now you want to ask students what was going on in "No Eight." Without knowing the significance of the first factor, 1.2345679, they will tell you that all the second factors were multiples of 9—in fact, the product of 9 and whatever specific favorite number was mentioned. You need to explain the importance of the first factor. Ask a student to write on the chalkboard the decimal equivalent for 1/9. Hopefully, a student will write "$0.\overline{1}$," a repeating decimal with a repetend of 1. So, 0.1..., 0.111..., and 0.111111111... are all names for $0.\overline{1}$. Take nine of the 1's, disregard the decimal point, and divide by 9 with paper and pencil. A basic calculator cannot display a nine-digit number. 111111111 ÷ 9 = 12345679. But to get an eventual product to fit in an eight-digit display, place a decimal point between the "1" and the "2." There is our mystery first factor, 1.2345679! So, 1.2345679 is the same as 11.1111111 ÷ 9 and when multiplied by a multiple of 9, e.g., 27 (9 x 3), the display will show all 3's.

"No Eight" is an interesting pattern based on a repeating decimal and a great way to start off "9 day."

As mentioned in the prologue, prepare pattern searches involving 9's on laminated oaktag and have cooperative groups move from each "booth" or station to the next. Prepare a lab report for groups to write their findings. "9 day" may become two or three days of working with patterns involving 9's depending on the groups' involvement with extended explorations. A critical part of this investigation is to have all groups report out their findings to the entire class. Here are a few patterns involving 9's for you to stock your "booths." (See Figure VI.2.)

Follow-Up

You do not have to limit pattern searches to the number 9. It is easy to use the number 9 as a focus for pattern searches; 9 is one of those

A. Fill in the blanks

1. $1 \times 9 + 2 =$ ____
2. $12 \times 9 + 3 =$ ____
3. $123 \times 9 + 4 =$ ____
4. $1234 \times 9 + 5 =$ ____
5. $12345 \times 9 + 6 =$ ____

See a pattern? Fill in the missing factors:

6. ____ $\times 9 + 7 = 1,111,111$
7. ____ $\times 9 + 8 = 11,111,111$

Include in your report all patterns observed.

A. Fill in the blanks

1. $1 \times 9 - 1 =$ ____
2. $21 \times 9 - 1 =$ ____
3. $321 \times 9 - 1 =$ ____
4. $4321 \times 9 - 1 =$ ____
5. $54321 \times 9 - 1 =$ ____

See a pattern? Fill in the missing factors:

6. ____ $\times 9 - 1 = 5,888,888$
7. ____ $\times 9 - 1 = 68,888,888$

Include in your report all patterns observed.

A. Fill in the blanks

1. $4 \div 99 =$ ____
2. $7 \div 99 =$ ____
3. $15 \div 99 =$ ____
4. $43 \div 99 =$ ____
5. $97 \div 99 =$ ____
6. $1 \div 99 =$ ____
7. $123 \div 99 =$ ____

See a pattern? Include in your report all patterns observed. Describe if and when the pattern "breaks down."

A. Fill in the blanks

1. $6 \div 999 =$ ____
2. $13 \div 999 =$ ____
3. $87 \div 999 =$ ____
4. $159 \div 999 =$ ____
5. $1 \div 999 =$ ____
6. $345 \div 999 =$ ____
7. $1234 \div 999 =$ ____

See a pattern? Include in your report all patterns observed. Describe if and when the pattern "breaks down."

Figure VI.2

numbers I refer to as a "neat" number. As you read journals and attend conferences, you will add to this collection and make "9 day" into a "9 week."

SUMMARY

In this chapter, two investigations were included that are favorites and make effective presentations. The study of patterns is a major focus of mathematics and is part of the mathematics curriculum from elementary to high school.

Obviously, the calculator is an effective aid in working with number patterns; it empowers students to delve more deeply into searches and not be impeded by burdensome computations.

There are geometric patterns in mathematics that need to be examined at all levels of the curriculum, too. They bring structure and order to the physical world. By studying these patterns and making the connections between arithmetic and geometry, students gain valuable insights into the structure of mathematics.

CHAPTER VII

Recreations

INTRODUCTION

Teaching mathematics is serious business but I also feel that the classroom should be a place where students and teachers can have fun; a place where students want to come because they enjoy math.

Included in this chapter are favorite "games" or recreations that can be used anytime during the school year. Depending on the skills involved, you may want to use them when teaching specific units within your curriculum. They reinforce both mathematics and calculator skills. I liked to use these recreations on "rainy Fridays," or, on rare occasions, when time remained in a class period. Once you use these recreations, your students will want to return to them during the year.

THE DIVISION GAME

Prologue

I first saw this activity in a book many years ago when we referred to "hand-held" calculators–how else would you hold them?–and have seen it many times since then. I have used it in the classroom and use it now in my workshops, usually when providing an example of the use of a calculator's division constant.

The activity will be described for use with a basic calculator's constant function for division. It will also work with the [Cons] key of the TI-12 Explorer or the [K] key of the TI-30 Challenger. By the way, although the TI-12 Explorer has a separate [Cons] key for use with repeated operations, the TI-12 Explorer works exactly as basic calculators with respect to automatic constants as described here. Did you know that?

Calculators such as the TI-108 and the MathMate–and yes, even the Explorer–have automatic constant capability for all four operations.

For division, if 14 ⊡ 2 ⊟ is pressed, the display reads 7. Then, if 10 ⊟ 24 ⊟ 6 ⊟ 9 ⊟ is pressed, the displays read respectively, 5, 12, 3, and 4.5. In the absence of a second number or divisor, the calculator "remembers" the original divisor (2) and the operation of division and divides each of the numbers, 10, 24, 6, and 9 by 2.

Use this activity anytime after students have worked with division of whole numbers and you have taught the use of the constant capability of the calculator.

Procedure

The key to playing this game is to teach the class a generalization. Once the generalization is taught and you demonstrate a few rounds of the game, you pair off students to play each other. Use the Overhead™ Calculator and a clear projectual to write down sequences so students can keep track of your work.

"Key in 8 ⊡ 8 ⊟."	Display: 1
"Key in 9 ⊟."	Display: 1.125
"Key in 14 ⊟."	Display: 1.75
"Key in 10 ⊟."	Display: 1.25
"Key in 17 ⊟."	Display: 2.125
"Key in 21 ⊟."	Display: 2.625
"Key in 15 ⊟."	Display: 1.875

You may want to include several more examples, but students should be ready to verbalize half the generalization you want them to know and use.

"If I divide any non-zero number by itself, what is the quotient?"
Desired response: "1"

"Now, look at each of the numbers to be divided. Describe them in relation to the divisor, 8."
Desired response: "They are all larger than 8."

"Now, look at each of these quotients when numbers larger than eight are divided by 8. Describe these quotients relative to the quotient, 1."
Desired response: "They are all greater than 1."

Now, with the constant division by 8 still active, go the other way.

"Key in 7 ⊟."	Display: 0.875
"Key in 3 ⊟."	Display: 0.375

"Key in 6 $=$."	Display: 0.75
"Key in 1 $=$."	Display: 0.125
"Key in 4 $=$."	Display: 0.5
"Key in 5 $=$."	Display: 0.625

In the same manner as above, you want students to see that when numbers less than 8 are divided by 8, the quotient will be less than 1.

Once the generalization is understood, you are ready to play the game. Turn your back so students cannot see the sequence you are keying into the Overhead™ Calculator. Try 13 $\div$ 13 $=$. Put the Overhead™ Calculator on the overhead. Students see a display of 1. You explain that you keyed in a number divided by itself. Their job is to guess your number. As a guess is given, you key it in and press the $=$ key. The number will be divided by your mystery number (13). Based on the quotient and what they remember about the generalization, they revise their guess upward or downward. This continues until a display of 1 is reached. A "1" in the display means that the number given is the same as your mystery number (13 ÷ 13 = 1). Here is a sample round.

Number giver (you): Secretly press 13 $\div$ 13 $=$ Display: 1
Class sees a display of 1 on screen.

First guess: 10
You press: 10 $=$ Display: 0.7692307

Second guess: 15
You press: 15 $=$ Display: 1.1538461

Third guess: 12
You press: 12 $=$ Display: 0.9230769

Fourth guess: 13
You press: 13 $=$ Display: 1
Bingo!

Demonstrate several games. The first time they try to guess your number and examine the display, they may use the wrong logic and go in the opposite direction when revising their first guess. After they get the procedure down, turn them loose. Pair off students. Each student secretly keys in: mystery number $\div$ mystery number $=$ and passes the calculator to the partner. Each guesser presses a number and the $=$ key, examines the display, presses another number and the $=$ key until a display of 1 is reached.

Limit mystery numbers to whole numbers less than 100 until they reach "expert level" and then take off the limit. With three-digit mystery numbers, the quotients will not change that much from guess to guess.

Follow-Up

Students get proficient with the guess-and-check problem-solving strategy as they home in on the mystery number. Good reasoning skills are also displayed. Sometimes students get lucky and a guess will yield a display of 2. What does that mean? The guess is twice as large as the mystery number—no further guesses are necessary. Or a guess will yield a display of 0.25. In this case, the guess is a fourth of the mystery number.

With the exception of lucky guesses, I tell students to "forget trying to do math, just guess!" The focus of the game is zeroing in on the mystery number by using logic and estimation skills. Try this one—your students will love it!

SHORT STUFF

Prologue

This "game" can be played at all levels and with any calculator. I like to use it after teaching students how to use their calculators; it is a good way of determining if they really can make "the keys sing." Some "nonbelievers" will say that this activity only reinforces use of calculator keys because it deals with key sequences, but do not believe them. Anytime you can engage students in an activity that involves mental math, estimation, and problem-solving skills–even if you are using key sequences—then you have a good mathematics activity.

The "game" can be played with any calculator and variations will be described for use with basic and advanced calculators. For a start, let us assume that we are working with sixth graders and a basic calculator like the TI-108.

Procedure

Set up a competition between individual students or teams of students. You are the referee and will rule on all disputes. For each round, students are given a target number and a digit or digits to use to build a sequence which will yield a target number in the display. The digits given must be used at least once and may be used repeatedly. Any operation key or feature of the calculator may be used. Students cannot use any digits that are not given. Students cannot use 0 as a placeholder unless it is given. The trick is to find the shortest possible sequence which will yield the target number. Every time a digit or operation key is pressed it is counted as a keystroke. The first individual or team with the shortest possible sequence wins the round.

Start with an easy one to ease students into the game.

Round 1:   Digits to Use: 2   Target Number in Display: 8

Hands will go up. A student triumphantly gives the sequence 2 ⊞ 2 ⊞ 2 ⊞ 2 ⊟. This sequence uses a total of 8 keystrokes, including the ⊟ key. Another hand goes up. This students remembers the automatic constant feature of the TI-108 and gives a shorter sequence 2 ⊠ ⊟ ⊟. This sequence uses four keystrokes and is a winner! Award a point to the student or team with the shortest sequence and proceed to Round 2.

A game of ten rounds will last a full class period with time for students to build sequences and provide for discussion. The discussion is important for students to explain their winning (shortest) sequence to the rest of the class.

Round 2:   Digits to Use: 4, 5   Target Number in Display: 49

Round 3:   Digits to Use: 6   Target Number in Display: 36

Round 4:   Digits to Use: 2, 4   Target Number in Display: 32

Round 5:   Digits to Use: 1, 7   Target Number in Display: 70

Round 6:   Digits to Use: 3   Target Number in Display: 81

Round 7:   Digits to Use: 5   Target Number in Display: 0.2

Round 8:   Digits to Use: 1, 2, 3   Target Number in Display: 44

Round 9:   Digits to Use: 3, 7   Target Number in Display: 100

Round 10: Digits to Use: 0,8   Target Number in Display: 792

Possible answers include: 2. 5 keystrokes, 45 ⊞ 4 ⊟;
3. 3 keystrokes, 6 ⊠ ⊟;   **4.** 5 keystrokes, 4 ⊠ 2 ⊟ ⊟;
5. 5 keystrokes, 71 ⊟ ① ⊟;   **6.** 5 keystrokes, 3 ⊠ ⊟ ⊟ ⊟;
7. 3 keystrokes, 5 ÷ ⊟;   **8.** 6 keystrokes, 32 ⊞ 12 ⊟;
9. 5 keystrokes, 3 ⊞ 7 ⊠ ⊟   **10.** 6 keystrokes, 800 ⊟ 8 ⊟.

With a scientific calculator like the TI-30 Challenger, students get to use all their calculator and mathematical skills. Here is a sample of five rounds.

Round 1:   Digits to Use: 5   Target Number in Display: 25

Round 2:   Digits to Use: 0, 9   Target Number in Display: 1

Round 3:   Digits to Use: 2, 6   Target Number in Display: 64

Round 4:   Digits to Use: 4   Target Number in Display: 24

Round 5:   Digits to Use: 8   Target Number in Display: 0.125

Possible answers include: **1.** 2 keystrokes, 5 $\boxed{x^2}$;   **2.** 3 keystrokes, 90 $\boxed{\text{SIN}}$ (Assume degree mode);   **3.** 4 keystrokes, 2 $\boxed{y^x}$ 6 $\boxed{=}$; **4.** 3 keystrokes, 4 $\boxed{\text{INV}}$ $\boxed{\text{EXC}}$ (x! is activated when $\boxed{\text{INV}}$ $\boxed{\text{EXC}}$ is pressed); **5.** 2 keystrokes, 8 $\boxed{1/x}$.

Follow-Up

You can modify the game to use with primary students or pre-calculus students. Depending on the calculator being used, students can get involved in some good mathematics.

As we move toward classrooms where calculators are available to all students at all times, playing Short is Better is one way to combine calculator and mathematical skills. You will be surprised at some of the sophisticated sequences your students will build as they work through the game. Some say the most elegant geometry proof is the shortest one; similarly, searching for shortest sequences by playing Short is Better helps students use their calculators with maximum efficiency.

MISSING FACTOR GAME

Prologue

Effective math games reinforce concepts and skills and, equally important, involve strategy. This game involves strategies with missing factors but the format could be used with missing addends, solving equations, missing exponents, etc.

This version of the Missing Factor game uses factors up to three digits and would be appropriate for middle and high school students. If single-digit factors are used, the game can be played with younger students. Mental math and estimation skills are reinforced in this game.

MISSING FACTOR GAME

___ x 83 = 1,411	36 x ___ = 1,296	49 x ___ = 2,496
___ x 6 x 15 = 8,000	___ x 21 = 411	8 x ___ x 64 = 1,024
___ x 65 = 2,345	___ x 16 x 5 = 6,400	71 x ___ = 2,343
9 x ___ x = 729	12 x ___ x 12 = 1,728	___ x 45 = 3,735
___ x 4 x 7 = 367	67 x ___ = 6,633	14 x ___ = 154
5 x ___ x 4 = 580	103 x ___ = 1,957	___ x 14 = 329
___ x 24 = 627	37 x ___ = 1,147	29 x ___ = 512
8 x 7 ___ = 504	___ x 7 = 686	115 x ___ = 736
29 x ___ = 1,189	99 x ___ = 1,089	___ x 52 = 1,118
2 x ___ x 9 = 198	6 x 3 x ___ = 794	___ x 117 = 938
___ x 65 = 6,498	___ x 505 = 6,060	9 x ___ = 1,184
11 x ___ = 699	___ x 24 = 1,341	75 x ___ = 5,625
___ x 13 = 169	4 x ___ x 8 = 288	4 x ___ = 277
413 x ___ = 2,065	___ x 989 = 5,931	___ x 42 = 1,764
	7 x 5 ___ = 345	

Figure VII.1

Procedure

This is a game for two students. It could be used in an interest corner for two students or played with the entire class working in pairs. The set of missing factor equations in figure VII.1 can be copied on large oak tag and laminated.

Player 1 picks a missing factor equation from the game board and circles it. If non-permanent markers are used, the circles can be washed off after each game. Player 2 now has ten seconds to guess, without using a calculator, the exact missing factor or an estimate of the missing factor. Have players use the classroom clock or provide a stop watch. Once Player 2 declares his/her choice, Player 1 declares his/her choice. An important rule—the second player cannot use the same number chosen by the first player. So both players have an opportunity to declare for each equation regardless of which player selects the equation.

Players now use calculators to find the missing factor. The player closest to the exact number scores a point. If either player selects the exact answer, two points are awarded. Now positions are reversed and Player 2 selects the next equation and circles it. The first player to score 15 points is the winner.

Follow-Up

Notice that in this game calculators are used solely to verify guesses. You may want to modify the time (ten seconds) before declaring a choice. Some students may need more time and some, less time.

Do not discuss strategy with students when they play the game for the first time—let them discover successful strategies. For example, if Player 1 is selecting and can use mental math to determine that the missing factor for 5 x __ x 4 = 580 is 29, then Player 1 will circle 5 x __ x 4 = 580 hoping that Player 2 will not chose 29. Good estimation skills are critical. Students will also use knowledge of multiplication and the relationship between the unit digit(s) of the given factor(s) and the product to make selections.

Students enjoy this game so much that you may have to make additional versions of the game so answers are not "memorized."

POWER GAME

Prologue

This game is included because of its similarity in format to the Missing Factor Game. It is appropriate for high school students; I used it when students were working with applications involving use of the keys on the TI-30 Challenger.

Procedure

This is a game for two students. It could be used in an interest corner for two students or played with the entire class working in pairs. The objective numbers for each round and set of expressions in figure VII.2 can be copied on large oak tag and laminated.

Both players examine the list of expressions and estimate which is

P O W E R   G A M E

Round	Objective
1	40
2	30
3	10,000
4	1
5	1,750
6	1,020
7	4,100
8	50
9	1,300
10	100,000
11	2,200
12	1,200

EXPRESSIONS

$$3^5 \qquad 6^4 \qquad 7^5 \div 7$$

$$40^2 + 10^2 \qquad 2^5 \qquad 13^3$$

$$(2^3)^4 \qquad 5^2 \qquad 5^8 \div 5^6$$

$$8^3 \qquad 2 \times (2 + 7)^5$$

$$(4^{0.5})^{10} \qquad 10^5 + 5^6$$

$$2^{17} \qquad 10^3 \qquad 6^3 \div 14^2$$

$$20^2 \times 10 \qquad 12^3 \qquad 36^2$$

$$15^2 - 13^2$$

Figure VII.1

closest to the round's objective number. Use a ten-second limit for students to make their choices. Choices are made without the use of calculators. Players then announce their choices and calculators are used to determine which player's expression is closest to the objective number. The player closest gets a point—as in the previous game, the second player to choose may not make the same choice as the first player. Alternate going first from round to round. Play proceeds to the next round. The player with the most points wins the game.

Follow-Up

As with the previous game, calculators are used solely to verify guesses. You may want to modify the time (ten seconds) before declaring a choice. Some students may need more time and some, less time.

Do not discuss strategy with students when they play the game for the first time; let them discover successful strategies.

You may want to make several versions of the game.

SUMMARY

Meaningful recreations or games have a definite role in the mathematics classroom. Skills and concepts are reinforced and strategies explored. Provide games for your students to play in your classroom. In addition to having fun and enjoying friendly competition, they will learn mathematics from the games in which they participate.

Word Fun

INTRODUCTION

Perhaps it is appropriate that this is entitled Chapter VIII, similar to the military's "section 8" designation for certain types of disorders. This stuff is corny, but it works with students.

Certain electronic digits in a display when viewed upside down resemble certain letters of the alphabet. For example, key in 317. Turn the calculator upside down. Now look at the display; do you see the word LIE? Corny? Yes, but it works in the classroom. Similar to use of the games in the last chapter, your students will have fun and be involved in mathematics.

These activities do have a function in the classroom. In designing activities with upside-down words, the teacher has built in a self-checking device. If a student computes correctly, then he/she will get a "word" answer. Use these activities after teaching students how to use their calculators. If "word" answers are not obtained, then students have to review their work to find their error.

Variations of "word" activities are included in this chapter. Depending on the skill level of your students, pick and choose the ones that are appropriate.

WORDS AND NUMBERS

Prologue

This activity involves addition and subtraction of three and four-digit numbers. Once students complete the activity, there are several extensions for students to explore.

WORDS AND NUMBERS

Match the "words" to the sentences.

1. I cannot tell a _____ .
2. He rang the _____ .
3. She put _____ on her bike chain.
4. The rabbit jumped in the _____ .
5. Mary climbed the _____ .
6. William's dad called him _____ .
7. Joan broke the _____ on her shoe.
8. Maria tried to _____ her old sled.

A. 967 − 257	**B.** 9036 − 1322
number _____	number _____
"word" _____	"word" _____

C. 6656 + 1079	**D.** 5414 + 2304
number _____	number _____
"word" _____	"word" _____

E. 243 + 74	**F.** 8793 − 1459
number _____	number _____
"word" _____	"word" _____

G. 9155 − 1417	**H.** 1863 + 1841
number _____	number _____
"word" _____	"word" _____

Figure VIII.1

Procedure

Students are provided with eight sentences, each having a missing word and eight computations.

Students do the computations using their calculators. A space is provided for the number answers and the "word" answers. They then place the "word" in the blank space in the sentence in which it seems most appropriate. Set up the activity with use of an Overhead™ Calculator. Key in the number 3507. Turn the overhead calculator upside down on the stage of the overhead projector. There is the word LOSE. In some cases, you will be mixing upper and lower-case letters, a small price to pay for a good math lesson!

Answers: 1. 317, LIE; 2. 7738, BELL; 3. 710, OIL; 4. 3704, hOLE; 5. 7714, hILL; 6. 7718, BILL; 7. 7334, hEEL; 8. 7735, SELL

Follow-Up

The above activity can serve as a springboard to a larger investigation. Have students determine those digits which produce "letters," 0 = O, 1= I, 2 = Z, 3 = E, 4 = h, 5 = S, 6 = g, 7 = L, 8 = B, and 9 = G. Using these "letters" have students make as many words as possible. Obviously, this word search is limited to the vocabulary of your students.

Give students a "word" and have them create an addition or a subtraction computation that will produce the "word." This is not as easy as it looks. See the next activity.

PROBLEM SOLVING WITH WORDS

Prologue

This activity involves missing numbers in computations with all four operations with whole numbers. Some of the problems are open-ended and engage students in problem solving.

Procedure

Students need to find missing numbers so that upside-down displays yield a "word."

Look at the first problem. The word is "BOSS" and the number that yields the word is 5,508. So, what number added to 2,921 will be 5,508? The number of digits in the missing numbers is provided for each problem. This is important because of the open-ended nature of some of the problems. Look at the sixth problem; the sum of the two numbers must equal 918, and each of the addends must be three-digit numbers. This disallows students giving answers like 917 + 1, 916 + 2, etc. Problem 10 involves critical thinking. There is a range of numbers that will work;

PROBLEM SOLVING WITH WORDS

Complete the computations to obtain the "words."

C O M P U T A T I O N	Word in Display

1. 2,921 + ___,___ ___ ___   **1.** ʹ8055

2. ___ ___,___ ___ ___ − 3,691   **2.** ʹ5hELL

3. ___,___ ___ ___ ___ x 9   **3.** ʹ6LO8E

4. ___ ___ x 551   **4.** ʹhI LL

5. ___ ___ ___ x 35   **5.** ʹSELL

6. ___ ___ ___ ___ + ___ ___ ___   **6.** ʹ8I 6

7. ___ ___,___ ___ ___ + 8   **7.** ʹBELL

8. 1,272 − ___ ___ ___   **8.** ʹLO6

9. ___,___ ___ ___ ___ − ___ ___ ___ ___   **9.** ʹhI 55

10. ___,___ ___ ___ ___ + ___ ___ ___   **10.** ʹhOE

11. ___ ___,___ ___ ___ + 17   **11.** ʹLE6

12. ___,___ ___ ___ ___ − ___ ___ ___ ___   **12.** ʹhOLE

Figure VIII.2

remind students that they are looking for a four-digit number divided by a two-digit number.

Answers: **1.** 2,587; **2.** 81,036; **3.** 4,231; **4.** 14; **5.** 221; **6.** any two three-digit numbers with a sum of 918; **7.** 61,904; **8.** 365; **9.** any four-digit number minus a three-digit number with a difference of 5,514; **10.** any four-digit number divided by a two-digit number with a quotient of 304; the range of the two-digit numbers is 10 through 32; **11.** 15,929; **12.** any four-digit number minus a three-digit number with a difference of 3,704.

Follow-Up

Once students complete this activity, they want to do more "word" problems. Create additional words and computations with missing addends or factors for your students to solve. Have students create the problems!

A TALL TALE

Prologue

A variation of the above is to create an entire story based on the upside-down "words."

This story involves computations which include parentheses and sums and differences of products. It is appropriate for middle school students and can be completed with a basic or advanced calculator. If students are using a basic calculator that does not adhere to the standard order of operations, then they will have to use the memory keys to hold partial results. As was said earlier, these activities can be used to review calculator skills. Remind students to "look before you leap." Many of the computations can be keyed in directly on a basic calculator like the TI-108.

Procedure

Students complete the story by filling in the missing words. Of course, the missing words are determined by completing the corresponding computations and turning the calculator upside down to view the "word." Students reinforce the use of order of operations and calculator skills as they do the computations.

Answers: **1.** 514, hIS; **2.** 491375, SLEIGh; **3.** 57738, BELLS; **4.** 34,

A TALL TALE

Complete this story by finding the missing words.

An old prospector was gliding over the snow in _____ _____. It

                                                           1.   2.

was a new model with six _____ attached to the runners. He was

                               3.

going so fast _____ made the snow _____. His _____ was named

             4.   5.   6.

_____ Smith. _____ told him to be in Fairbanks on time so he could

7.   8.

_____ _____ skins to the highest bidder and pay off all his _____.He

9.   10.   11.

decided to make this _____ run because of the danger involved.

                           12.

Just then he hit a _____ _____ and fell to the snow. He began to

                   13.   14.

_____ around in the snow but thought better of it. "I'm too _____ to

15.   16.

trudge through this stuff." He took out an _____ and began to _____.

                                 17.   18.

His tragic tale was later made into a movie called "The _____ and

                                                         19.

_____."

20.

1. 24 x 17 + 106 **2.** 2948250 ÷ 6 **3.** 685 x 96 − 8022

4. (2652 − 34) ÷ 77 **5.** 587 x 986 − 2113 x 99 + 2620

6. 297432 ÷ 54 **7.** 1782 + 31 x 31 x 31 **8.** 4550 ÷ 13 − 5

9. 221 x 35 **10.** (35600 − 134) ÷ 69 **11.** 56 x 99 x 13 − 14354

12. (10 − 3.655) ÷ 9 **13.** 18 x 51 **14.** 62 x 19 + 817 x 8

15. 601 x 75 **16.** 566080 ÷ 16 **17.** (350 − 19) x 3

18. (30000 − 215) ÷ 37 **19.** 18 x 23 + 193 x 3

20. (2 x 19 x 19 +3) ÷ 25 − 28

Figure VIII.3

hE; **5.** 372215, SIZZLE; **6.** 5508, BOSS; **7.** 31573, ELSIE; **8.** 345, ShE; **9.** 7735, SELL; **10.** 514, hIS; **11.** 57718, BILLS; **12.** 0.705, SOLO; **13.** 918, BIG; **14.** 7714, hILL; **15.** 45075, SLOSh; **16.** 35380, OBESE, **17.** 993, EGG; **18.** 805, SOB; **19.** 993, EGG; **20.** 1, I

Follow-Up

Now you are ready for a student project. Invariably, your students will comment on the corny story. Have them create a story about the same length of A TALL TALE. Once they try to put one of these together, they will appreciate your literary talents. Share student stories with the class and award a literature prize for the best one as judged by the class.

CROSSWORD POWER

Prologue

Word fun has many variations. Here is a crossword puzzle with words obtained from upside-down displays. This puzzle uses all four operations with whole numbers. If you look at the computations, even though they include some parenthetical expressions, they all can be keyed in directly on a basic calculator. So, depending on vocabulary level of students, this activity is appropriate for students who have worked with all four operations.

Procedure

By now, you know what to do with these "word" puzzles. Students do each clue's computation using their calculators, then turn the calculator upside down and read the word answer.

Answers: Across **1.** 3504, hOSE; **4.** 137, LEI; **5.** 491375, SLEIGh; **8.** 38, BE; **9.** 5309, GOES; **11.** 34, hE; Down **1.** 304, hOE; **2.** 7735, SELL; **3.** 4914, hIGh; **5.** 335, SEE; **6.** 993, EGG; **7.** 3379, GLEE; **10.** 40, Oh

Follow-Up

If any of your students are crossword junkies, they may tell you that this puzzle does not have symmetry—professional crossword puzzles have a line of symmetry—a diagonal, where one side of the puzzle's blocks is a mirror image of the other side. Your answer to these astute

Crossword Power

Even if you don't like to do crossword puzzles, you'll like this one. That's because you don't need to know the word clues below. Use you calculator. Do each clue's computation, then turn your calculator upside down and read the word answer.

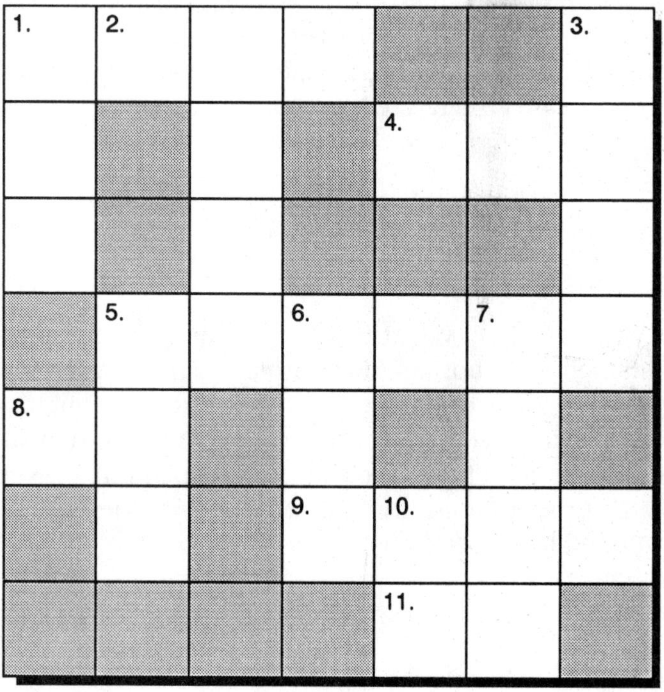

Across

1. Squirts water 219 x 16
4. Garland 3288 ÷ 24
5. Type of sled 3931 x 125
8. Exist (1467 – 23) ÷ 38
9. Leaves 37163 ÷ 7
11. Pronoun (1910 – 6) ÷ 56

Down

1. Garden tool 19 x 2 x 8
2. Vend (1540 + 7) x 5
3. Lofty 13 x 27 x 14
5. Look (2100 ÷ 6) – 15
6. Breakfast food (299 + 32) x 3
7. Mirth (30600 ÷ 9) – 21
10. Exclamation (2543 – 23) ÷ 63

Figure VIII.3

observers is for them to create crossword puzzles that have symmetry using computation clues and upside-down words!

TONGUE TWISTERS

Prologue

Just when you thought the list of variations was exhausted, here are some tongue twisters—all based on upside-down words in calculator displays. Though some of the computations involve squares of numbers, all of them can be keyed in directly on a basic calculator. Several of the computations involve decimals.

Procedure

By now, if you have used previous activities in this chapter, students know what to do.

The fun part of this activity is when students try to say each of the tongue twisters five times—quickly.

Answers: Commas and apostrophes have been added for clarity. A. ELSIE'S ELIGIBLE. B. LO, LOB LOOSE LOGS. C. SOLO, ShE SOBS SIGhS. D. BOO BOB'S BOSS E. SEE SIS SELL ShELLS. F. BLESS BLISS, BEGS BILL. G. SOL, SEIZE ZOO SLEIGh.

Follow-Up

It is hard to follow-up an activity on tongue twisters. I have had students try to create additional tongue twisters using the upside-down "word" bit but there are a finite number of possibilities. Some of the ones in this activity are from students. Students like this activity and the self-checking feature of working with upside-down "words."

SUMMARY

This chapter contained activities which used the motivational technique of obtaining "words" in a calculator's display. Like the chapter on recreations, the focus is on learning mathematics and having fun. Use these types of activities as you teach students how to use their calculators. These activities are self-checking; if a "word" is not obtained, then a mistake has been made.

I have "spiced up" algebra lessons by taking advantage of this technique. In solving a set of equations using calculators, students would

Tongue Twisters

This sheet contains tongue twisters but you can't see them, they're disguised. You have to do some math first; with your calculator, of course. Do each computation, turn your calculator upside down and the answer in the display becomes a word. Put the words in the blanks and you'll have seven tongue twisters. Try saying each one quickly–five times. Bet you can't!

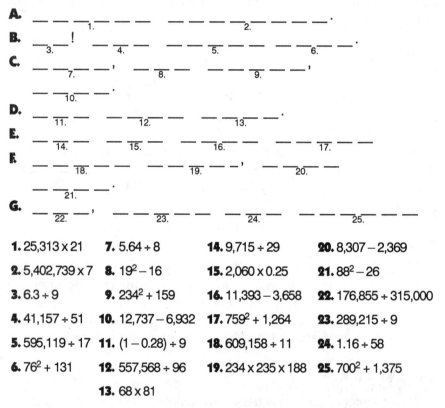

1. 25,313 × 21

2. 5,402,739 × 7

3. 6.3 ÷ 9

4. 41,157 ÷ 51

5. 595,119 ÷ 17

6. $76^2 + 131$

7. 5.64 ÷ 8

8. $19^2 - 16$

9. $234^2 + 159$

10. 12,737 − 6,932

11. (1 − 0.28) ÷ 9

12. 557,568 ÷ 96

13. 68 × 81

14. 9,715 ÷ 29

15. 2,060 × 0.25

16. 11,393 − 3,658

17. $759^2 + 1,264$

18. 609,158 ÷ 11

19. 234 × 235 × 188

20. 8,307 − 2,369

21. $88^2 - 26$

22. 176,855 ÷ 315,000

23. 289,215 ÷ 9

24. 1.16 ÷ 58

25. $700^2 + 1,375$

Figure VIII.3

sum their solutions. This sum would yield an upside-down "word." If students did not get a word, then one or more of their solutions was incorrect.

Try word fun with your students. Once again, you may be surprised at your students' creativity.

CHAPTER IX

Some Final Words

A LOOK AHEAD

This book has been about teaching mathematics in classrooms in which calculators are readily accessible. The activities in the chapters involved students in rich investigations and explorations with a focus on problem solving, estimation, mental math, and number sense. A major thrust of this book was to show teachers that "good" mathematics can be taught in classrooms where students have total access to calculators.

This book has also been about change; change in attitudes toward calculator use and change in how mathematics is taught when teachers take full advantage of the power of calculators.

Technology is constantly changing and teachers must be prepared to use new technologies as they become available. We now have a basic calculator that processes operations according to the standard order of operations, calculators that accept, display, and manipulate fractions, and more powerful graphing calculators which provide users with greater power to graph functions and solve equations.

What's next? Who knows? The above products would have seemed far fetched several years ago. In workshop discussion groups, I ask teachers what they will do in a few years when calculators or small computers are built into students' desks. Far fetched? I do not think so. The point is that we must be prepared to use any technology and new developments that will help us effectively teach mathematics to our students.

The NCTM Standards has provided us with a vision of how mathematics should be taught in the 21st century. The use of calculators is critical in helping us achieve the goals outlined in the Standards. The activities contained in this book will aid you as you use calculators to teach mathematics. I hope you enjoy using the activities in this book as much as I have enjoyed using them in classrooms and workshops.

SUGGESTED READINGS

National Council of Teachers of Mathematics. Curriculum and Evaluation Standards for School Mathematics. Reston, VA: National Council of Teachers of Mathematics, 1989.

National Council of Teachers of Mathematics. Professional Standards for Teaching Mathematics. Reston, VA: National Council of Teachers of Mathematics, 1991.

Fey, James T. editor. Calculators in Mathematics Education, 1992 Yearbook. Reston, VA: National Council of Teachers of Mathematics, 1992.

Mathematical Sciences Education Board and National Research Council. Reshaping School Mathematics, A Philosophy and Framework for Curriculum. Washington, DC: National Academy Press, 1990.

ADDITIONAL SOURCES

Bobis, Janette F. "Using a Calculator to Develop Number Sense." Arithmetic Teacher. Reston, VA: January, 1991.

Pagni, David L. "Teaching Mathematics Using Calculators." Arithmetic Teacher. Reston, VA: January, 1991.

Williams, David E. Calculator Corkers, Sets A, B, C. The Calculator Workshop, Abington, PA: 1986.

Williams, David E. The MathMate Activity Book, Levels 1, 2, 3. Stokes Publishing Company, Mountain View, CA: 1992.

Zollman, Alan. "Low Tech, 198, and the Geometry of the Calculator Keys." Arithmetic Teacher. Reston, VA: January, 1990.